To Father Jack,
Their intelligence isn't artificial.

Robert Schwartz

Smart Humans? Smarter Animals

Smart Humans? Smarter Animals

Robert S. Swiatek

for pet owners, those who work at rescue facilities or zoos and scientists studying our four-legged friends

Table of contents

Introduction

In November 2010, my book, *Save The Animals And Children*, was published. Sometime before that, a friend said I should write a children's book but I figured I couldn't. That changed in late 2010 with my really short book about creatures and the environment – especially that of where I live – written by Wendy the woodchuck. When people ask, I tell them *Save The Animals And Children* is a sophisticated children's book about really smart animals. So is this one. It's also about heroes, the environment, communication, devotion and caring.

Over the last few months I have seen programs on television and read quite a few books about smart elephants, orangutans, parrots, cats and dogs, who also display feelings and use intuition. Those five species are only the beginning of the list. Chantek the orangutan may not be able to talk like you or me, but he knows sign language. He knows it well, even creating his own symbols. He probably can curse in it. He's so smart that he uses tools, emulates Felix Unger, and can tell you where your car is parked so you can take him to the Dairy Queen. Moreover, he leaves his trailer at night – I think he has a date – and to get through the chain link fence, unravels it. Eventually he fixes it so that no one can tell that he escaped that way. Chantek is one smart great ape.

Before he died, Alex the African Grey Parrot was famous. He could talk, just listening to humans. He recognized colors and did simple math. When getting the answer wrong, he was just showing that he was bored, which Greys experience quite often. Alex really knew the right answer. Another Grey was named Charlie Parker. His owner, Deborah Smith, encountered an obnoxious insurance agent on the phone and wasn't making much progress. She was quite frustrated. Charlie heard her and sympathized with her. Sounding exactly like Deb's husband, Michael, the bird offered a few off color remarks, even though he was a Grey.

An eagle named Freedom arrived at a rehabilitation center where Jeff Guidry became his caretaker and saved his life. Months later, the eagle would return the favor. This story is as incredible as the tale of Andre, the seal pup rescued by Harry Goodridge of

1

Rockport, Maine. Harry took care of Andre, and the seal left the area there and headed out into the ocean. He always returned, even if it was days later. Winter was a challenge for Andre so Harry was fortunate to place the seal at the New England Aquarium for the cold months. The first trip there by car wasn't pleasant for Andre so Harry let him swim back in the spring. He managed to find his way to the Goodridge place, which he did yearly. Even when Andre was losing his vision, he still managed the journey.

You'll read about Aisha and Echo, two elephants who managed well with people as well as their families. A few dogs I talk about are Boo, Ace, Sergeant Rex, Oogy, Marley, Barney, Katie and Pransky. Some you may have heard of. Dewey and Oscar show off their skills as felines. Spirit Bear, Wesley the owl, Otter 501, Christopher Hogwood and Clyde the cassowary – not his real name – are a few others along with their keepers that I'll familiarize you with. I'll also mention some creatures that people stay away from or just don't like. In many cases, the feeling is mutual, and I don't blame the animals.

For some time I've never doubted that many creatures possessed *intelligence* despite not being able to talk – Alex and his buddies are the exception. I'm not getting into the definition of that word, but only say that over the last few months I've come to acknowledge that walruses, sharks, emus, crows and pigeons are equipped with brains and may have more smarts and feelings than many humans. Some scientists don't believe that animals have common sense, intelligence or can feel emotion. This book might convince them and doubters otherwise.

One of the words in my title needs some consideration: *smart*. Combining it with another word or two creates an oxymoron in many cases. It wasn't long ago that we were introduced to *smart bombs*. If they are so *smart*, why do we have collateral damage when they land on hospitals and schools? Wouldn't doctors, nurses, the wounded and students be still alive if these bombs were *smart*? More recently the *smart phone* appeared for sale. I doubt that this item is *smart* since the majority of the people say that the cell phone is the worst invention ever. If I can't find my phone, why doesn't it tell me where it is if it's so *smart*? Another off-the-wall use of the word is with the body part that we sit on. Perhaps that phrase should be coupled with another one that

2

we hear quite often, *She – or he – has a nice* ▓▓, which seems reasonable because you can talk to it since it's *smart*.

Returning to my four word title, the first half might be an oxymoron in too many cases as proven by the warning given at Yellowstone National Park to not take selfies with bears. This was recently reported on *National Public Radio*. Apparently, that advice is necessary. *Smarter Animals* is fine since a comparison is involved. Additionally, owners of pets, those who work at animal rescue facilities or zoos and scientists studying four-legged, crawling, swimming and flying animals are *smart* people. It is my hope that when you finish reading my book you'll agree that my title is quite appropriate.

The photos on the book cover are from top to bottom and left to right: Alex, Barney, Freedom, Su-Lin, Christian, Dewey, Chantek, Seabiscuit with jockey Johnny *Red* Pollard, and Christopher Hogwood. In a few cases the pictures are of trained actors.

bobcooks.com

1. Honey

At one time, I had a record album of Bobby Goldsboro's greatest hits. The LP is gone but I copied it to a cassette. Many of the songs were sad, including "Honey," which was a number one hit, selling a million copies. This chapter is about that sweet substance, starting with an animal that loves that sticky stuff.

Looking at him you'd think Stoffel would make a great pet. Then he opens his mouth. The teeth of this honey badger look vicious. Stoffel isn't really a badger, but a weasel, *Mellivora capensis*. He loves honey and belongs to the same family as badgers: *Mustelidae*. Otters, minks and wolverines are all relatives. Honey badgers can be found in India, Southwest Asia and Africa. Stoffel is fearless and such a great escape artist that he might put Dean Gunnarson to shame. Stossel even inspired a 2011 YouTube video, *Honey Badger Don't Care*, which received more than 60 million views. He was the star of that production. There are many videos of those critters, and he probably isn't in all of them.

Stoffel's residence is in Kruger National Park in northeastern South Africa. Instead of the word, fearless, perhaps a better description of this critter is ferocious. He'll tangle with any animal in the jungle, but probably not an elephant. Stoffel isn't afraid of lions, even though the latter could easily end a honey badger's life. In the process, the king of the jungle would receive quite a beating. The lion would just back off from Stoffel, especially hearing his roar and seeing those powerful teeth. The little guy also has terrifying claws. Stoffel has another challenge from the hyena, but most will move away from this weasel and depart. Even with a few accomplices, a group of hyenas will usually retreat.

Snakes hardly bother Stoffel, even poisonous ones sinking their fangs into him. The weasel even takes the crawling critter home for dinner, but only one of the animals remains in sight after dessert. Stoffel may have to overcome the poison in his body, so he won't be roaming far and wide until he recovers, which he does. The poison he accumulates may be just the immunization he needs, without the sting of the needle. As you can see, a honey badger is carnivorous and has few predators. He's one tough dude.

Spotting a honey badger, you might think it's a very large skunk, because of the white streak on top of his back and head. While the latter is also known as a polecat, the two animals have the common practice of perfuming the area but in no way is it a pleasant experience. It probably should be regulated. Stoffel and skunks may be half cousins once or twice removed, which is what you should do if spraying begins. The polecat has a weapon that humans and pets fear because of the problems of removal of the stench, which is just as difficult as it was for Jerry Seinfeld after his car was perfumed. The good that skunks do is remove grubs and they won't bother you unless provoked, but then, you should run. Those honey badgers missing the characteristic skunk white are of the *Cottoni* subspecies.

Photographing Stoffel is a challenge since he's always on the go, probably a type A. Honey badgers and humans seem to keep their distance, the former figuring the woman with the camera has a gun hidden somewhere. At the Maholoholo Wildlife Rehabilitation Centre in Kruger Park, conservationist Brian Jones cares for wounded weasels and rehabilitates them. He wonders whether there is any enclosure that can fence Stoffel in. His attempt at confinement consists of cement blocks, but the trees inside it offer a way out for the captive. Stoffel bends them and crawls out on them.

Jones removes all but one of the trees, which is in the middle of the pen. Stoffel then breaks off the branches and constructs an escape ladder. There's no stopping him. He always finds a way out. Putting an electrified fence seems to be the next step, but Jones doesn't want to harm the guy, who is some smart animal. His problem solving ability is amazing. I need not remind you that those scary looking claws can dig underneath and provide an escape. Even if you built a cement block enclosure with a concrete floor and cover that Stoffel couldn't get through, he'd probably find a jackhammer and discover freedom.

At a lodge in the park, zoologist Low de Vries does a night surveillance of honey badgers and other animals scavenging for food at the dump. Grownups as well as pups, who stay with their mother for two years, are on the scene. Porcupines are also dumpster divers, but no challenge for the honey badgers. The others are discouraged when the mother badger lets loose her perfume. Low de Vries is far removed but still affected by the stench. Even entering his car doesn't help much.

In a lodge in the park, beekeeper Guy Stubbs has the assignment of keeping honey badgers away from their love, that golden substance. He works on a few ideas and some fail, but he tries again. This time Stoffel is stifled. However, his girlfriend, Hammy, looks like she is on her way to the honey, which she soon reaches. Then Stoffel joins her. In getting to the treasure, the pair is stung repeatedly, but they'll just sleep off the hundreds of stings. There's no need for any immunization now.

It was a similar honey harvest that resulted in Stoffel having 300 stings and in need of rescue, which Brian did. The honey badger was in distress but was relieved when Jones calmed him down with Hammy. You can see more about Stoffel and his friends on the PBS *Nature* special, *Honey Badgers: Masters of Mayhem.*

If you've seen the early episodes of *Saturday Night Live*, you may be familiar with John Belushi and the wolverine. Not only was this skit on the premiere performance of the show, it was the very first one. After it ended, Chevy Chase appeared in the scene with the words, *Live from New York, it's Saturday Night*. That was on October 11, 1975, and the program was officially, *NBC's Saturday Night*, eventually becoming *Saturday Night Live*. Chase didn't fall down on that first show, which would come later. Getting back to the wolverine and John, who played an individual learning English, he repeated whatever his teacher said, portrayed by Michael O'Donoghue. This included the line: *I would like to feed your fingertips to the wolverine*. As you can guess, the bit is on the Internet. To find it, search for *Belushi and the wolverine*.

Wolverines may be more ferocious than honey badgers since they're much larger. Also known as carjarou, skunk bear and glutton, the wolverine is a distant cousin of Stoffel and Hammy, especially due to where he resides – northern Canada, Siberia, Alaska and northern Europe. A few years ago, a few were seen near Lake Tahoe and are known to be in Michigan. A solitary member of the *Mustelidae* family, wolverines like the cold, unlike the honey badger, who'd rather be in Africa, where it's warmer. I think the moniker, *glutton*, is unjustified as wolverines can't find that much food where they reside to ever have lavish banquets.

7

Carjarou manage the extreme cold because of their thick fur. Their legs may be short, but the paws – similar to that of honey badgers – allow them fast movement through the tundra. The quicker you move, the warmer you stay. If they were gluttons, they could never employ such quick movement. These animals aren't dumb. Approaching the size of a Belgian sheepdog, the male wolverine is almost a third larger than the female of the species and can weigh as much as 70 pounds. The only family member that's larger is the otter. Like the skunk, these creatures can liven up the air with an unbelievable stench, which they utilize for protection. They have few predators, but wolverines ignore the warning to *pick on some animal of their own size*, which doesn't worry them. They don't mind if their dinner is still in motion. Some of supper choices are elk, adult deer, porcupines, rabbits, beavers and moose. They must call in other relatives to share the moose. Carjarou probably don't care for bear meat but will stand up to bears and wolves to defend the carrion the wolverine acquired. Their diet can be dead, alive or frozen. To complete their food pyramid, these fearless animals also feast on the eggs of birds as well as on berries, the larvae of insects, seeds and roots.

Like the honey badger, wolverines move fast and avoid being seen. No terrain is an obstacle to them, even steep cliffs, and they don't need carabiners and pitons. They cover an area of about 500 square miles, sharing it with their relatives – but probably not third cousins. Because of their elusiveness, not many researchers study them. They try anyway and if they have any luck, their observations are from a distance. Doug Chadwick has been a fan of them for years, observing them in the wild. He comments: *Like most of the guys on the project, what I really want to do is just be a wolverine. I want to go where I want to go, do what I want to do, bite whom I want to bite, and climb what I want to climb.* Apparently he's not opposed to uncooked frozen food.

Filmmaker Steve Kroschel has spent a quarter of a century pursuing wolverines. Like the care and concern of Brian Jones for honey badgers, Steve works with injured as well as abandoned wolverines in Alaska. Kroschel has raised a pair of orphans since they were born and it hasn't been easy. Nonetheless, he manages because of his devotion to the two as a surrogate parent. There aren't many people in the world who perform this generous act. There's more information at his web site, www.kroschelfilms.com. You can also watch the PBS *Nature* special, *Wolverine: Chasing the Phantom*, which aired in November 2010.

Every letter in the word, *wolves*, can be found in the word, *wolverines*, but they're not exactly related. Coywolves evolved when coyotes and wolves started dating, and it wasn't through Facebook. They can be found in eastern North America and identified as red wolves, eastern coyotes or eastern wolves. Throwing in foxes, these species are probably all distant cousins in some way. There's another animal that's a more obvious relation, but that's for later. Many of these species have gotten a bad wrap, as witnessed by the 1983 movie, *Never Cry Wolf*. There the wolves were blamed for killing off the caribou herds, when they were just going after the weakest of the herds and thinning them out. The caribou probably would have died anyway, so this action actually strengthened the herd. Wolves do the same with other animals, specifically sheep. If you haven't seen the flick, I highly recommend it. It's a humorous, environmental motion picture that's insightful and worth a few stars. Tyler, the two-legged scientist played by Charles Martin Smith, was a true hero and friend of the earth – except for his culinary meal choices. However, we can excuse him since he was running out of food. His scene underwater was scary, but his beverage choice was all right.

Many farmers and hunters think that predators are harmful to cows and sheep, but ridding a region of wolves can be more of a detriment as has been recently shown. Their absence may lead to a preponderance of some species that devour plants and shrubs that cows may feed on. The result is beef that may not be grass fed and unhealthy for human consumption. In the ecosystem, predators are needed for so many reasons – this includes the two-legged kind.

Packs of wolves once could be found from the tundra of Alaska to as far south as Mexico. By the early 1960s, habitat loss and extermination changed that in most of North America. In the early 1970s, the Rocky Mountain wolf entered the list of endangered species and Greater Yellowstone became one of three recovery areas. In the mid 1990s, over 40 wolves from Montana and Canada were introduced into the national park, which became a wolf research area. The animals have spread through Yellowstone and continue to help the ecosystem.

Allen Boone encountered an animal that most people avoid. Zephyr was a skunk that lived by day in the woods, so he wouldn't be shot and then roamed the neighborhood at night for gourmet food. The others couldn't get him because he was smart and Boone befriended him. You have to unless you don't mind baths of tomato juice. Allen respected him so much that Zephyr went through the garbage with the human close by and then made himself at home within a few feet of Boone. It continued when Zephyr introduced his family to Allen.

This impressed him deeply. When he went to a meeting in Los Angeles on human relationships, he offered the suggestion that these connections should not be limited to humans. The subject of skunks came up, but many didn't feel the same way about them as Boone. One dissenter raved on about skunks' nuisance capabilities and left snorting. He was a lawyer, but a few days afterwards apologized to Allen after a bit of research, saying, *I know relatively few humans that I consider fit to be called skunks.*

Bill Bezanson spent his early life on a farm in Romeo, Michigan, in the middle of the twentieth century. There probably weren't any wolverines or honey badgers on the property but maybe some wolves. The family had two barns so Bill was allowed to use part of one for rescuing animals. He cared for foxes, possums and even a skunk – he didn't douse Bill since he was smart. Bill also helped a raccoon, whose mom was smacked by a car. His siblings didn't make it, but Pierre LaPoop did, named by Bill's grandmother.

Pierre was kind, devoted and loved by Bill. They even played together, even though Pierre was wild. The mischievous animal could fish without a pole, shuck ears of corn, ransack garbage and open doors without a key. Once when the family came home, Pierre was tossing plates in the kitchen. He thought he was a juggler. He also washed his hands a lot in the rain barrels. Seeing this, Bill's dad threw him into his truck and drove him a couple dozen miles away, where he left him.

A few weeks later, Bill and his father were fishing when Bill saw a raccoon up a tree and called out, *Pierre, is that you?* The animal came down and showed his affection to the lad. Bill's dad

10

accepted Pierre back into the homestead since he didn't have funds for a plane ticket.

LaPoop grew up and departed. He found a wife through a dating service and the pair had four little ones. Bill and his dad found this out because Pierre brought his brood back to show them. Father and son held each young raccoon. When done, the family of raccoons left and moved into the woods. Pierre had just come to say good-bye.

I'll have more to say about my garden in Elma. I had two raccoon encounters, though I didn't see any of them on either occasion. The first occurred in Plainville, just outside of Syracuse around the time of my summer corn roast. I grew quite a few vegetables, so the day before the event I went to see if the corn would be ready. It looked real good. The day of the party I saw quite a few of the corn stalks on the ground. The raccoons had beaten me to the punch. Fortunately they left some so I didn't have to buy any that day. The previous year I didn't experience that problem because the farmers planted feed corn all around me, something that wasn't done the year of the raccoon raid.

A few years after that in another suburb outside Buffalo, I couldn't grow corn unless I wanted to feed the wildlife. For that Saturday corn roast I bought corn at a farm stand – it was out of this world, as always. After people had eaten, the garbage bags were filled and I had to remove it to the recycling / landfill place, which wouldn't be open until Tuesday. I placed the bags inside a six-foot high area surrounded by a chain line fence. Before long, some raccoons got to the refuse after hopping the fence.

Just as most people see Pierre, his relatives and my visitors as an annoyance, many feel the same way about squirrels. In late spring of 2014, I was about to watch a PBS *Nature* special about pelicans in the outback, but realized that I had already viewed it. Instead I watched a *The Nature of Things* feature on the CBC. It covered squirrels: red, brown and gray ones. The program began with a guy who was set to nuke their neighborhood as he was fed up with the critters. I'll say more about him in a while.

Scientists had a project to determine if squirrels were smart enough to find the acorns they buried. I'm not sure where I came up with the idea that those critters buried the nuts so they could dig them up when they were hungry months later. This is not the case as squirrels have to stuff themselves to survive the winter – thus they do the burying and then the finding and eating within a short span. Another consideration is that even with a shovel, it's hard to dig up frozen ground.

The first task of the experiment involved planting tracking devices in the acorns. Next a single squirrel – let's call him Sam – had to take the bait. That is, he had to bury a few of the doctored acorns. He was then captured and moved to another place for a few days. With him away, observers checked to see if other squirrels would dig up the bounty, but none did. Either it was out of respect or they had their own cache to uproot. It should be noted that when Sam did the initial burying, he may have done some pretend digging and then placed the acorn in a different spot underground. This wouldn't be a problem for the observers.

When Sam came back, he went straight to work and located the buried acorns. This he did by triangular tracking, combining mathematics and the location of objects in the surrounding area to reach the nuts. Sam was one smart squirrel. He wouldn't starve over the winter.

Squirrels have such finesse among the trees, gliding from one branch to another. If it looks as though they are flying, that's because they are. You may think that these creatures ascend the tree by moving up it. In essence, they remove both sets of legs at once and fly a short distance. All along we thought differently about what they do.

Red squirrels may be predominant in one area, but not gray ones. The latter could be close by, though. Surprisingly this results because of the humans and the way they live. Think of the fear of one type of squirrel, which may not be sensed by another. So if a red squirrel doesn't worry about howling canines while a gray squirrel does, the environment changes accordingly.

In England, red squirrels and gray squirrels don't co-exist together because the latter carry a virus that kills off the red squirrels. One solution may be to kill off the gray ones, but it's rather cruel. One scientist is working on creating a vaccine to protect those in danger of the virus. This is a much better option. Humans who brought the squirrels from America are to be blamed for the problem.

When I lived in Elma a dozen years ago, I had to protect my garden from deer, raccoons and woodchucks, which I somehow managed. I was fortunate to not be bothered by squirrels since they could easily hop any fence. A chain link fence wouldn't stop them and the garden would have to be fenced in above and completely covered with chicken wire. I didn't have fencing on the top, but there were squirrels around since I lived near plenty of trees. In the spring on my property and the empty lot next door, numerous saplings broke through the ground, including maples and oaks. The latter indicate that the squirrels around were planting acorns, but not retrieving all of the acorns. The squirrel could have had enough to eat or maybe a predator got him. There were more maples sprouting than oaks, but I surrounded the young plants with fencing to protect against deer, woodchucks and rabbits that would devour them otherwise.

Getting back to our avenging resident from a few paragraphs ago, he's come to his senses. He figures the animals were here before him, so why not coexist. If his resident gray squirrels like some of his flowers, he can do without them, planting others that animals won't touch.

Certain animals belong to different families, but they're all rodents: gophers, beavers and woodchucks, who are also known as groundhogs, whistle pigs, or land-beavers. Of the lot, the beaver is the greatest friend of the environment, despite what many people think. Those that hate the animal want to hunt and kill that industrious creature because of the floods that he causes. These men with guns even resort to blowing up the animal's dam. Others just bulldoze the dams. Much to their dismay, it would soon be rebuilt, even overnight and the destroyers would probably say, *damn*. At least the beaver didn't mine their homes.

Those who don't approve of the work of any beaver just don't realize what he or she can do for areas where water is in short supply. For now, suppose the beaver's name is Bucky. Researchers out west noted that a stream there was barely visible, maybe an inch deep. When Bucky came there and began his project, it wasn't long before there were ponds with water five feet deep, lush growth and animal wildlife. This is exactly what the scientists wanted the animal to do.

As far as flooded areas or those about to be inundated with water, Bucky had to be persuaded to build dams in the appropriate places. One gentleman environmentalist tried a few things. With some effort and ingenuity, he managed to have Bucky build the needed structures and kept the water in check, without paying him. Bucky didn't ask for supper breaks or benefits either. Had the Army Corps of Engineers been called in, local residents would have had their taxes increased.

Beavers – *Castor fiber* in Europe and *Castor Canadensis* in North America – have been around for four million years, and some of their relatives even before that. Living in the United States and Canada, they once numbered in the hundreds of millions, but more recently that has been reduced to about nine million. Hunting and trapping for their fir caused the decline. Canada is noted for its wilderness and yet these two efforts nearly made the beaver extinct. The beaver is the Canadian National symbol. I'm not sure why that is. Was it because of the furs or the environment?

It's miraculous that they still inhabit the earth but that should be no surprise since my words on destroying their dams and fast reconstruction earlier illustrates their determination. They're tenacious and tough as they come, having survived climatic and geologic changes over time.

Wherever beavers are active, you can find water. Even in periods of extreme drought, the species can change the landscape and bring the water by their activity. Scientific studies showed that with beavers, ponds had nine times more water area than those without them. Beavers once were a third of the size we see today, when they weighed about three pounds. There was one close to nine foot long. I wonder what he fed on – anything he wanted. If he battled the hunters and trappers, I wouldn't place any bet on the latter.

Timber – truly a great name – was an injured one-year old given to the care of Michele Grant. Because beavers are family oriented, Michele wanted to provide love to him, but not too much so Timber could be released back into the wild. They touch noses as a sign of affection, which his caretaker experienced. Grant swam with him and his progress was slow, at first staying underwater for a few seconds and then a minute. This creature can be underwater for fifteen minutes at a time. Beavers are vegetarians, eating leaves and branches. Eventually Timber graduated to the latter and one day was gone. Michele searched for him without any luck and after a few weeks she found a beaver skull and was sad. A bit later she was at a neighbors pond when she saw Timber. He had survived and even had a wife and family. Because beavers are faithful, Timber never had to worry about alimony payments.

Beavers build winter residences – an elaborate underground network in the water of the pond. They store plenty of branches for the cold months and their residence for that time is more like a hotel, since other rodents join them and don't pay any rent. They all exist in harmony. Beavers are foresters, felling trees for the dams they construct. I've never seen a beaver on the Ellicott Creek Trailway, but I've seen a stump without the rest of the tree confirming their presence. Beavers work in construction, but they don't create subdivisions that displace wildlife. Lastly, they're the greatest environmentalists of all the animals. You can read more about these amazing animals in Glynn Hood's book, *Beaver Manifesto*. Another informative, entertaining beaver treatise about Archibald Belaney and Anahareo is the book, by Anahareo, *Devil In Deerskins: My Life With Grey Owl*. Archie is also known as Grey Owl.

2. Hound Dog

Most people are familiar with the song written by Jerry Leiber and Mike Stoller that was a number two hit for Elvis Presley in England. It did better in the United States, reaching the top spot on both the pop and country charts. Big Mama Thornton recorded it in 1952 and it became a hit for her the following year. This chapter is about smart, loving canines.

He was only a puppy, but he had been beaten up and abandoned on the railroad tracks on January 9, 2012 near Hackney Marsh and Leyton. Who was responsible for this cruel act was not known, but some kind soul contacted Nigel Morris in the control room close by. He set out to look for the dog, an Anatolian Shepherd, designated as Stray: E10. Nigel met a stranger with two dogs, who seemed a bit unusual, but he proceeded to search as the guy left the area. Then he located the animal, who was covered with blood, suffering but was surprisingly calm. It was almost as though the shepherd realized that Morris was there to help him. Nigel contacted the RSPCA for assistance while he stayed with the dog.

Driving in her Citroën Berlingo, Siobhan Trinnaman came to help and met Morris. The trains were still running and Siobhan was distraught when she heard a train approaching. Nigel assured her that the dog would be fine, knowing just what to do, flattening himself to avoid any further injury. The woman noticed that the injured animal had damage to the tail and one of his legs, besides being roughed up. Despite this, the gentle giant was good-natured and welcoming to his rescuers. Carefully, they carried the animal to her van and Siobhan drove him to *Harmsworth Memorial Animal Hospital* in North London.

Hospital director, Stan McCaskie, also saw how calm and relaxed Stray: E10 was despite his extensive injuries. Unfortunately, animal cruelty was quite prevalent in England with so many strays. The shelters did their best to find good homes for the rehabilitated dogs, but sometimes they had to resort to the dreaded PTS (Put To Sleep). After the pooch had settled in his kennel, Michelle Hurley of *All Dogs Matter*, a charity rescue service, was one of the first to see him.

17

A guy who worked with Michelle thought that a good name for the shepherd would be Haatchi, and others agreed. In the early 1920s, a Japanese Akita dog with the name Hachikō, was so dedicated to his owner, Professor Hidesaburo Ueno, that he waited each day at the train station for him. His name referred to the dog's birth order with his siblings and also meant *prince*. When Ueno was stricken with a hemorrhage at the University, he never came home. Still Hachikō returned each day to wait for the teacher, being at the station until he himself died. Besides the similarity in their names, what the two dogs had in common was the train. This loyalty came out in a 1987 film in Japan and eventually in the 2009 movie, *Hachi: A Dog's Tale*, starring Richard Gere.

Anatolian Shepherds date back 6,000 years. They are descendants of Mastiffs and also known as Turkish Shepherd Guard Dogs, used to herd and protect sheep. Possessing great hearing and sight, these dogs are known as *lion hunters* – they must be tough – and canines don't come much larger. Though he was only a puppy, Haatchi had to recover from the assassin's meanness first. He lost most of his tail and one leg, but luck was with him. Rescue centers combined with technology to spread the word and he avoided PTS, at least for a while.

All Dogs Matter's Ira Moss approached Lorraine Coyle, who cared for dogs in Hendon and Coyle. She was pleased to take care of Haatchi until he found a permanent home. The puppy and Lorraine's twelve-year old boxer got along well, but Haatchi would move on. Eventually he was situated at *Dogs And Kisses* in Oxfordshire, run by Ross McCarthy and James Hearle.

Owen Howkins was born on August 25, 2005 to Will and Kim Howkins. Each was in the armed forces and had assignments in war zones. Luckily, both Kim and Will had supportive families who would look after Owen. When Owen was staying with Will's parents, both Bill and Joan Howkins mentioned to him that his son didn't seem right. When Kim's parents, Sara and Hugh Knott, agreed with that, Will and Kim thought the lad should see a specialist. Dr. Neil Thomas diagnosed that Owen had Schwartz-Jampel syndrome, type 1A, caused by a gene mutation. It's a myotonic condition in which muscles are stiff and weak, causing problems in bone growth. It meant the young boy would be confined to a wheelchair or walker and need medication. With his parents away so often, life would be much more challenging.

Because of all the stress, Kim and Will's marriage suffered, so they sought counseling. They wound up divorced. They would care for Owen separately and the lad went around with his head looking down because of his condition. Colleen Drummond was divorced but friends posted her picture on the Internet. She and Will were in cyberspace contact and soon met in person. They felt comfortable with each other, but more important, she loved the child and said he was her *Little Buddy* – hence the name *Little B*. Owen was also fond of Drummond. Will's parents were accepting of Colleen, too.

In January 2012, Will's new love was going through the pages of *Dogs And Kisses* when she saw the picture of an Anatolian Shepherd. Mr. Pixel was a collie-spaniel mix that joined two of Colleen's working dogs in the household, but the shepherd captured the hearts of Will and Colleen. That gentle giant was Haatchi. When Haatchi spied Colleen, his tail was doing the wave, the first time he did that in some time. Soon after that, Will woke his son with a big surprise. Seeing the shepherd caused Owen to open his mouth wide, followed by Haatchi quietly placing his big head on the child's leg. On seeing the massive animal, Owen's life was changed. He had been shy and struggling at school, but he was happier, outgoing and now doing very well in school. Eventually he learned what had happened to Haatchi and talked all about it to others. Another life was affected. A quote by Gene Hill says it all: *Whoever said money can't buy happiness forgot about puppies.*

At *Dogs And Kisses*, the mighty giant had been fed a raw food diet so Will and Colleen thought they would continue doing that with Haatchi. Colleen called *Natural Instinct* and ordered food that would satisfy the big canine. She received a call soon after in which Suzanne Brock stated that they wanted to sponsor her dog, providing him with free food for life. Watching his friend eat healthy food, Little B starting doing the same. Haatchi also inspired Owen to take all his pills, just as the dog was doing.

The Anatolian Shepherd waited for Owen to return from school. On the first day, Haatchi wandered the house looking for his buddy. Little B talked to others freely and he and Haatchi helped raise money for numerous causes, even helping with the

Howkins' medical bills for the lad and the canine. Both of them became well known and they won numerous awards for bravery and perseverance. They didn't even enter into these competitions. Owen no longer kept his head down as he had done and took Haatchi to school. He was a big hit there. The painter Sara Abbott commented on the dog: *It is as if he is a human in a dog's body. He just seems to understand everything.*

The monster dog touched so many lives. A lady in a prone position in a wheel chair spotted Haatchi and her smile was enough to light up London. A little girl in Southampton followed the canine on Facebook and when she was in the hospital for surgery, Haatchi visited her there, lifting the girl's spirits. At first the authorities blocked his entry into the room, but soon allowed the big guy in. The shepherd was in training in the United Kingdom as one of 5,000 *Pets As Therapy* dogs. He also sang and danced to cheer up the depressed, anxious and elderly.

Colleen and Will planned to be married and found a place at Barton's Mill. Everything was there that they needed. In order to make the decision on the venue, they had to obtain the approval of Owen and Haatchi. The dog and his buddy agreed when the four of them were at the site. But then the dog was trembling and tense and Will and Colleen felt it could have been something he ate. They heard the noise from a passing train and they knew. They let Haatchi get through the trauma by himself – something that Colleen knew as a dog trainer – and the shepherd managed. In the days before the wedding, Colleen and Will took Haatchi back to the train area and the dog was fine, since he was one smart canine. On Saturday August 17th, the couple was married. Their two *children* were there and had the greatest time.

The person who had beaten and left Stray: E10 on the tracks to die didn't realize how he had affected so many people. His plan to extinguish the Anatolian Shepherd's life didn't quite work out but did bring comfort, joy and love to people throughout the world. Haatchi would eventually need more surgery, which he managed quite well. However, viewing the results caused the vet to say that more might still be necessary. It may have been avoided through hydrotherapy, which the dog dove right into. As a result, he was spared going under the knife, at least for the present.

When I finished reading the book on Owen and Haatchi as the last days of summer approached in September 2014, PBS had a fourteen-hour, seven day special on the Roosevelts. In many ways that family and the Howkins family were very similar. Each one had members that were deeply wounded – suffering physically, mentally and spiritually – but they overcame this. Theodore, Franklin and Eleanor comprised the most influential family in American political history. Both families endured wars and made a great impact on others. Ken Burns produced *The Roosevelts: An Intimate History*, so it was top-notch. The book on the Howkins family is *Haatchi & Little B: The Inspiring True Story Of One Boy And His Dog* by Wendy Holden. The author of the following fitting quote is unknown:

He is your friend, your partner, your defender, your dog. You are his life, his love, his leader. He will be yours, faithful and true, to the last beat of your heart. You owe it to him to be worthy of such devotion.

Glenn lived in a suburb of Buffalo with his family and at first was fearful of dogs. A spotted English pointer name Strippy, who howled ferociously while chained to his doghouse, may have been the cause. When Glenn was four, the menace on four legs broke loose and came upon the lad and his six-year old sister, pushing them down. The two were terrified, but Strippy was just happy to see them and be free. Unfortunately, too many people want pets, procure them but then leave them alone and chained. A few years later a beagle named Lady changed Glenn's mind about canines. It was quite a while before he decided that maybe it was time for a dog.

He wrote for magazines and newspapers as well as the book, *Horowicz: A Biography Of Vladimir Horowicz*. Living in a dark apartment on the Upper East Side of New York, Glenn felt he needed a better place to live. Battery Park City, built on water at the tip of Manhattan, seemed like a good choice. It wasn't really a huge houseboat, but a village built with what was excavated from the building of the World Trade Center in the middle of the twentieth century. The Hudson was drained and filled in to build a 92-acre environment, complete with an Esplanade, hotels, museums, schools, stores, marina, housing and great views of Lady Liberty in the harbor. The complex had over 1,700 apartments in six buildings and over 300 dogs.

Glenn moved into a place on the third flood and one hot summer day, his friend Michael suggested that he get a dog. The latter chose Baby, a cute pug, and Glenn paid for the pooch. Brought to his apartment, their relationship was exactly like a one-night affair as he brought Baby back to the pet store a day later. After a year had gone by, Joe, a longtime resident of Glenn's building brought up the dog deal and mentioned Dinah, his three-year old cocker spaniel. Glenn still wasn't sure so he asked if he could borrow Dinah as an afternoon test-run dog. The results were satisfactory, so Twiggy, a cocker spaniel puppy, wound up in the writer's home. Arriving back home, they met Nancy, a neighbor, with a green wing macaw on her shoulder, Mojo, who said, *Pretty girl, pretty girl – want some chicken?* Eventually, the spaniel would delight when she heard the word, *chicken.*

It wasn't long before the puppy had a new name: Katie, named after Katherine Hepburn, her master's favorite movie star. By this time Glenn had met Pearl and Arthur, his neighbors in 3C, whose dog Brandy had died a short time before. When Katie came to see the couple for the first time, they were thrilled. They liked Glenn too and the feeling was mutual. Because of various circumstances, Arthur and Pearl were surrogate grandparents for the writer and he in turn was the child they never had. Glenn often referred to Katie as his child and there were quite a few people who could spoil her. Glenn's housekeeper, Ramon, hated dogs and threatened to quit but his friend said that Katie wouldn't bother him. Ramon stayed and the two got along fine.

Glenn took Katie on interviews, even when dogs weren't allowed in the building. He snuck her in and all adored her. Her presence may even have landed him an assignment at the *Daily News.* Katie had many fans besides Pearl and Arthur, including Glenn's grandmother Essie, aka Nana. They saw each other very often at Thanksgiving. Katie was very therapeutic for Glenn, Arthur and Pearl and they returned love to the spaniel. The canine wasn't happy with small dogs and was hesitant with children. Maybe they were just too fidgety. She got along well with large dogs and adults. Walter, the Belgian quarter horse that policeman

Sean rode on his rounds in Battery Park City, quickly became friends with Katie. Having been raised on a farm with dogs had something to do with the affection between the two.

Katie joined the fashion world, modeling sweaters for the *Daily News. Family Circle* came calling next as the dog did a spread on summer picnics, complete with fried chicken. In an almost similar way, not to be outdone, Glenn became a theater participant in a spoof of *The Wizard of Oz* after he joined a community center. I have more on that shortly.

Katie may have been precocious, but she listened and learned. She didn't understand every word that others said, but she knew many of them, besides chicken. These included the usual sit, stay, listen up, go out, no, treat, cookie – probably not kale and kohlrabi – ball, cake and what are you doing? She knew some commands so well that one time when Glenn took her into pet-friendly *Bergdorf Goodman* on Fifth Avenue, she knew what he wanted when he said, *Katie, SIT. Good girl. Now Staaaay.* A customer saw the dog and asked, *How much is that?* The businessman thought Katie was a stuffed animal. A very similar event occurred on the subway – where dogs weren't allowed. This time the person asking about buying Katie appeared to be a rapper and Glenn imagined a possible mugging. Katie wasn't sold, no harm was done and from that point on, Katie and her master rode in taxis. Following rules was a good idea.

Katie was very gentle with people who were suffering from body pain. She recognized Arthur's arthritis in his legs so she never came up on them. She showed her respect for Freda, a retired judge with braces necessitated by earlier polio. On seeing the magistrate, the spaniel offered a paw. Katie treated Pearl as though the latter was her mother. She had great devotion to Nana, but when the latter died at 91 of cancer, Katie went to the funeral, comforting Glenn's mom. She did this all night long. With the death, Pearl took Nana's place.

Life had been perfect for Glenn as he interviewed Al Pacino, Meryl Streep, Nancy Reagan, Katherine Hepburn, Elizabeth Taylor, Audrey Hepburn, Leona Helmsly, Barbara Walters and many other celebrities, even writing a book on them. In January 1993, the *Daily News* was sold to the *Tribune Company* and Glenn lost his job. His associates at Battery Park City were a great comfort to him but then during a winter snowstorm, his back gave out, resulting in spasms and pain. He was depressed and in need of help.

He went to a community center in Greenwich Village and discovered their social events and services. Bringing Katie along, the spaniel and father met Ryan, a three-year old boy. Surprisingly Katie and the lad bonded, even though she was hesitant at first. They were soon running after each other and having a wonderful time. Glenn ran into John, the boy's dad and soon learned that Ryan loved dogs. The two adults and Ryan were soon living in the same building in Battery Park City, on the same floor. Katie was there too. John and Ryan were residents in 3P.

Once they moved in, John mentioned to his new friend that there would be a blessing of 3P. He invited Pearl, Arthur, Katie and Glenn. The ceremony was a long-lost tradition of Christian and Jewish culture. When it was held at sunset, an Episcopal priest joined the group with some of John's friends in a circle, hands together. They were celebrating family and community. Katie was on a leash but well behaved. Arthur offered a Hebrew blessing. This blended with the Episcopal reading.

> *Graciously receive our thanks for this place...and put far from those who dwell here every root of bitterness, the desire of vainglory, and the pride of life. Turn the hearts of the parents to the children and enkindle fervent charity among us all, that we may evermore be kindly affectioned one to another. Amen.*

John went to work but Ryan was in good hands with Arthur, Katie, Pearl and Glenn. On one occasion when the writer was with the lad, the youngster started sobbing. The adult comforted Ryan assuring him that he loved him, as did his father John, who would be home soon. For reinforcement, Glenn brought a smile on his face when he bought Ryan a strawberry ice cream cone. Katie enjoyed some of the ice cream too. One day Ryan and Katie encountered an eighty-pound Labrador retriever at the elevator in the building. Fang seemed to be threatening the boy until Katie stepped in. Growling, the protector did her job as the aggressor backed off. They had many great times together, running after each other up and down the hall chasing a ball tossed by Glenn. This endeavor produced two sleepy *kids* at night.

The writer's loss of work and his health problems landed him in bed with depression but slowly he improved in mind and body. His support team had much to do with that, as did his therapy. One day he decided to head to the session on his bike, three miles away. He was close to home when a crack in the pavement sent him flying off the bike, landing on his face. He was on the concrete and couldn't move with a broken nose, cuts and other injuries when a Samaritan came by to help. Plaskin was soon on his way to *St. Vincent's Hospital*. With the accident, his depression was starting to end, brought about by something he had read a while ago: *A grateful heart can never be a depressed one.*

It wasn't long before Glenn had visitors, including Katie, who Pearl snuck in. She stayed with him under the covers. A surgeon doctor came by and said that he would reset his nose without anesthesia. It would hurt, but the process would work. It did and miraculously, he was released from the hospital that same day. Recovery would take some time, but the people and dog on the third floor would get him through it.

Time passed and in the late 1990s, Glenn was writing again, this time for *Family Circle* as a free-lance writer. The grind of a newspaper and the interviews were gone. Arthur had died and there was more bad news – John and Ryan were moving uptown to a new place. On the day of the departure, Katie jumped on Ryan's lap, somehow knowing that he wouldn't be around with him to run up and down the hall. The event also affected Pearl and Glenn deeply. In the days that followed, Katie would be going to 3P, looking for John and Ryan, who made occasional visits. It wasn't the same. Pearly had lost a son and grandson; the cocker spaniel, two friends; Glenn was missing his friend and his son.

Tuesday, September 11 was a beautiful summer day in the first year of the 21st century – for a while. Glenn heard an explosion but felt it was due to all the construction in the area. When Pearl called him, he knew disaster had struck. He told her he'd meet her in the lobby as he went for Katie and his cell phone. When he got downstairs, she wasn't there. With all the falling debris, visibility in Battery Park City was limited and Katie was suffering. A policeman helped and the dog was herself again.

People were headed to safety in New Jersey on police boats close by. Meanwhile Pearl was rescued by Lee, a financial planner, who finally convinced Pearl to step into the Jersey bound boat, but not without much reluctance. Many people from Battery Park City stayed temporarily with friends in New Jersey, including Pearl who shared the home of relatives, but wasn't happy there. Glenn and Katie moved uptown into John and Ryan's apartment.

Slowly people moved back to the buildings in Battery Park City, but not all did, even abandoning their furniture. Katie grew old, with arthritis. She was hard of hearing, almost blind and in much pain. Glenn's friend Paul convinced him that it was time for Katie to be put to sleep, affecting Glenn and Pearl deeply. Pearl was slowing down too and her diverticulitis brought her to the hospital. Social Services found a full-time aid but she didn't work out. Finally, Naia, a Russian aide came on the scene. She and Pearl were great friends and Lee visited almost every day as well. She was progressing slowly when diverticulitis struck again. Pearl was back in the hospital once more and died there at 3 a.m. on October 18, 2004.

Glenn's *family* on the third floor of the building was gone with John and Ryan in Paris. He was depressed but soon realized that what they had there had been something truly special, and it probably would never be repeated. He still lives in his apartment in Battery Park City and has met others who fill the void. You can read more in Glenn Plaskin's book, *Katie Up And Down The Hall: The True Story Of How One Dog Turned Five Neighbors Into A Family.*

3. This Cat's on a Hot Tin Roof

A few months ago I read a book about some amazing felines. It's kind of a sequel to a book that you've probably heard about referring to cat named Dewey, thanks to Vicki Myron. I haven't read *Dewey: The Small-town Library Cat Who Touched The World*, but I did read *Dewey's Nine Lives: The Legacy Of The Small-town Library Cat Who Inspired Millions*.

It all started on a frigid night in January 1988 in Spencer, Iowa. The temperature was brutal at fifteen degrees below zero when a deposit was made in the book return slot of the library there. It wasn't a book, music or movie, but a tiny kitten who stayed in the cold metal box for anywhere from ten hours to a day or more. When Vicki Myron opened the return receptacle, she saw a freezing eight-week old pussycat. She warmed him up as best she could, including a soothing bath followed by drying with a blow dryer. The little guy showed his thanks by pressing his nose against each staff member there. He acquired the name of Dewey, probably because someone suggested the connection to the library classification system.

His full name became *Dewey Readmore Books* and he fit right in to the place. Spencer was facing a farming crisis and the town needed something. Vicki was new in her position at the branch and Dewey saved her just as she had saved him. This same give, take and give back occurred time and again in the Spencer library. The number of patrons increased and the staff had a change of attitude. Things in town would never be the same. A really great thing had happened.

Dewey made people in the building feel good and he certainly didn't mind the attention. He wasn't partial as he was cozy with anyone nearby. Shy people petted him and soon knew about his night in the box – even those who weren't cat lovers. When Dewey did readings and signed autographs, the crowds were overflowing. Obviously he was a smart guy, but come on, he couldn't read or write even though books surrounded him.

Crystal was a student who had physical disabilities. She only stared at the floor but then the library feline headed for her wheelchair as she rolled along. Crystal began making sounds and before long, a smile covered her face when she caught a glimpse of him. Dewey and the children had a special relationship, and he especially loved babies. When he came near them, they may have petted him and tugged on his ears. He didn't mind. Dewey may have napped a great deal, but the children all knew him as he spread love and joy to young and old alike.

One gentleman wrote that after his divorce, without Dewey, it would have been hard to go on. The feline restored his heart. A woman with muscular dystrophy read Vicki's book and moved to the floor to kiss her dog. She rose from there without assistance. Sadly, her dog died shortly thereafter. Across the ocean, a British man had lost his wife a few months before and read the book about Dewey. Only then did he see that the two cats she left behind carried him through his sadness. There are other numerous instances of Dewey's influence on people, which you can read about in the two books I mentioned earlier. You will also find tales of many other cats in *Dewey's Nine Lives*. What follows is another story.

Sioux City, Iowa, is less than a hundred miles from Spencer. Glenn Albertson grew up there and was six foot four and two hundred sixty pounds at eighteen, playing on the football team, naturally. Not long after graduation, he married and had a son. Glenn pumped gas and repaired automobiles. Simultaneously, he trained to be a policeman. He later had another son and a daughter. One day Glenn brought his daughter home from Sunday school, and one of his friends answered the door. His marriage was over.

He took on all kinds of work, being a bouncer and bartender. He even sold insurance. He met an elderly gentleman, who had lived through the Depression. The latter advised him: *Learn as much about many things as you can, because that way you will never have trouble finding a job.* Glenn was appreciative of the advice and actually had been practicing that himself, as his list of jobs showed. He knew carpentry, plumbing and electricity. After a few years, he married a waitress and they moved to St. Petersburg, Florida.

He soon discovered that his new wife was doing the cheating thing. He married a third time, a friend he had known for years. The couple couldn't have children, so they decided to adopt. In the process, they took in foster children, but unfortunately they left for some reason or another. They decided to adopt Jenny, a full-blood Sioux. Albertson's third wife left, too, taking Jenny with her.

One day, Glenn was under the dashboard working on a car when something like a fur ball fell onto his stomach. It was a white and orange cat, about six weeks old. He soon had the name of Rusty. They became good friends, but Rusty wouldn't come to Glenn's house, at first. When the cat was five, he weighed about twenty-five pounds. Jenny and Rusty got along fine.

Glenn spent evenings attending divorced dads' meetings and drove to dances to hear music. He may even have played his guitar at times, if asked. He soon played more often at *Storm'n Norman's Rock and Roll Auditorium*. He handled chores there, too, such as carrying the keg, tending bar and unclogging toilets. One thing he didn't do was dance, until one night. He spotted her and noticed the glow so he headed over to her. When he asked her to dance, she agreed. For now, we'll call her, Ms. M, and she had health problems, including walking. She figured she could handle one dance, especially since the guy was so handsome. Somehow she did fine on the dance floor for more than a single dance.

Ms. M's husband was a drunk and they had gotten divorced. Both Glenn and Ms. M liked each other, sharing much of their lives. As might be expected, neither wanted another marriage. However, they were suited for each other so they moved into the same house. They each had a cat in their lives, but the one in Ms. M's life had died. He had been a library cat named Dewey. Ms. M was none other that Vicki Myron. You can find all the details about these relationships in her books about Dewey.

Thanks to Myron, the whole world knew about the cat in the library in Spencer. Her book was a best seller in Portugal, Korea, Brazil, England and China. When Dewey died, he had lived nineteen years. His obituary was printed in the Sioux City paper and ran in almost 300 newspapers. Fans signed his condolence books by the hundreds. His memorial was attended by the same amount. Letters from around the world were sent to the Spencer library and for months, librarians were approached by reporters and others to learn more about Dewey. Dewey was laid to rest outside near the wing of the children's library.

In the late 1970s, pet therapy barely existed. At the *Steere Housing and Rehabilitation Center* in Providence, Rhode Island, which dealt with dementia and Alzheimer's patients, Henry lived in the building as it was being constructed, so he stayed. He was a stray cat named after the benefactor, Henry Steele, and the feline remained for a decade. He was such a force that half a dozen cats replaced him over time. In the twenty-first century, the tradition was repeated, but one stood out: Oscar. He wasn't named after the wiener, I don't think.

Oscar visited many of the residents, but usually didn't remain long in the room. If he stayed, it meant that death was close at hand – most likely that same day. If a resident was moved to the hospital and about to leave this planet, Oscar would hang out in the room where the resident had been. He did this often. At times, after someone had died and Oscar spent time in the resident's room, staff noted that Oscar seemed in need of a vacation – tired and worn out. Obviously it affected him.

Dr. David Dosa was the resident physician and he was aware of the feline's skills. His scientific background made him question Oscar's talent. Was the latter really that attuned to the suffering of the residents? He witnessed and talked to family members. He knew of many instances of this great cat's work. David wondered what Oscar would do if two people were dieing at the same time. It did happen, so he would go to one and then the other as soon as he could.

Ida mentioned her cat, Patches, always knew when Ida's arthritis was bothering her or when she was ill. On those occasions, the feline would stay with her while other times – when Ida was fine – Patches was nowhere to be seen. Maybe he went to the track. Sadly, Patches died of cancer. Kathy said that Oscar was in the room for her mother, but he soothed Kathy just as well, maybe more so. Oscar relieved her of her loneliness at a troubling time, making her realize that the feline knew exactly what was happening. This occurred again and again.

Dosa would write a book about Oscar. *Making Rounds With Oscar: The Extraordinary Gift Of An Ordinary Cat* is an amazing story. Oscar took up residence in the nursing home but wasn't there because he was collecting social security or suffering from an accident. He had concern for the patients. Cats may not all have nine lives, but they do have a sixth sense, and Oscar exemplifies that by his love for the residents. He performs a service, without pay – all right, he gets some cat chow and is finicky. Oscar didn't care whether you were rich, poor or what your background was. He was there for the people – staff, residents and their families. This is just like the good done at various Hospice places by therapy animals. Dosa's book is about a one-of-a-kind cat, nursing homes, dementia, Alzheimers and the transformation of the author, who really got to know Oscar. Many words describe his book, but perhaps the most fitting is remarkable.

Jenna is another remarkable cat who lives in Buffalo. Len, a Eucharistic minister from St. Joseph University Church, told me about this tortoiseshell kitty. Also known as a tortie, Jenna is mostly black and carmel. She's a hunter, maybe related to the panther since she has brought rabbits to Len. My cat Jaspurrr also brought me presents, but they were mice and birds. Jenna is one tough cat as she can get her prey even when she's on a leash. You would think the bunnies would learn to stay away.

I need to pass along the tale of a really cool Siamese, named Koko. This dude is the main character of Lilian Jackson Braun's novel, *The Cat Who Talked Turkey*. All right, so it's fiction, but it's an amazing and amusing story of a smart Moose County journalist, Jim Quilleran, and his pets. Koko's partner in crime is Yum Yum. Some people overlook the intelligence of four-legged creatures, but clairvoyant Koko's insight might convince these doubting Thomases otherwise. Braun has written more enjoyable novels regarding Quilleran and the pair of Siamese.

Returning to the real world, Anthony *Ace* Bourke and John Rendall left Australia and settled in London in the late 1960s. They went to *Herrods' Department Store* and saw two lion cubs there, one male and one female, and thought they would buy the former, which they did. His name was Marcus, but it didn't seem quite right so Ace and John decided on Christian. It had something to do with Christians being fed to the lions. Before they picked up the cub, they had to make sure that the accommodations were adequate.

Their apartment was too small, so they found another place, the building where they worked. It housed a shop called the

Sophisticat, which seemed fitting. It had a huge basement so the only other search was for a large garden where Christian could roam. Friends provided that. During the day, Christian would sit on the furniture in the shop window. One day someone mentioned that a child saw the cub and said to his mother, *Mummy, there was a lion in that shop window.* His mother replied, *Don't be ridiculous. If you don't stop this lying, I'll get your father to thrash you.*

Christian, the guys and their associates got along fine, respecting each other. Those who ventured into the shop when Christian was there didn't have to have stitches. The lion was smart and didn't want to lose a customer. He could open the basement door without a key. If there was food stored high up, it didn't stop him as he knocked it down to get it. Naturally Christian grew and John and Anthony knew that they would have to have their four-legged friend liberated and transported to Kenya, or some wildlife area before he became too domesticated.

They had a few worries about shipping him off. Christian would have to be in a cage for about fifteen hours for the journey from London. Would he be all right? The next concern was his ability to make it in the wild. He landed in Kenya a bit tired and groggy, but what human doesn't feel that same way after such a long flight? Ace and John discovered that Christian adapted quite well in his new home.

On a later visit to Kenya, John and Anthony couldn't seem to find their lion friend, but then the two and Christian saw each other. He stood still, but then moved slowly towards them, eventually leaping into their arms in a show of love and devotion. This relationship was a fine example of a slight modification of the familiar thought, *They laid down with the lion, and all got some rest.* The change of scenery was good for Christian, but that was the last time the two saw him. He may have met his end because of predators with four legs or those with guns – animal poachers. On the other hand, a lion lives into his twenties and Christian may have just died a natural death, since he was no longer a teenager at this last reunion.

Besides the YouTube video, which millions have viewed, there was an *Animal Planet* special called *A Lion Called Christian*, and many other programs that you'll find by doing an Internet search. You can also read the book by Bourke and Rendall, *A Lion*

Called Christian: The True Story Of The Remarkable Bond Between Two Friends And A Lion.

The 1965 movie, *Born Free*, is also about a young cub, Elsa, who grows to adulthood under the watchful care of a young couple. She had a more difficult time adjusting to being in the wild, as all she wanted to do was play. That may be because of her sex. As a result, the other creatures not only gave her a rough time, she almost doesn't survive the beating they bestowed on her. After a while, she attacked a warthog and they're both at the dinner table, except that Elsa is the only one dining. *Born Free* is supposedly a true story, but it's based on a novel. That doesn't mean that most of it didn't really occur. Insofar as Christian was real with a similar background and assimilation issues, there's no reason why we can't believe that Elsa lived on the planet.

Brian Setzer was a member of the Stray Cats for a while – certainly appropriate for this chapter. Later this guitarist, singer and songwriter became the leader of the swing band, The Brian Setzer Orchestra. It's still active and features five saxophones, four trumpets and four trombones. One of the group's releases was *The Dirty Boogie*. "This Cat's on a Hot Tin Roof" is from that CD.

4. Stewball

Living in the Rockies, naturalist Joe Hutto saw wildlife every day. Herds of mule deer appeared not far from his house so he approached them slowly since they usually stayed away from humans. He was out every day for over two years when a very nervous doe cautiously approached him. Through Raggedy Ann, the boss of all the others, he gained entry into the herd. It wasn't long before all the members accepted him. Joe was now a mule deer. Ragtag, Raggedy Ann's daughter, became pregnant and Joe talked to the soon to be born fawns as he lied down with the mother. This was a special privilege for Joe, who then was accepted by the twins, a buck and his sister Molly. Some people might ask why he had continued doing this and he replied, *How could you not?* As close as he was to the group, they would scatter when other humans came on the scene.

After a while Hutto knew the deer and they knew him. Boar was the largest buck, but Babe was the male in charge – the dominant one. Blossom was a doe. Mule deer don't ordinarily groom each other, but Ragtag groomed Joe. Sadness descended on Joe and the deer when Molly's brother died one night. Ragtag was especially distraught, staying with the young buck, never overcoming her depression. She died too. Molly was alone and then sustained an injury. With winter coming on, she would have a tough time surviving.

Fortunately, Blossom helped out and Molly seemed to do fine. Other deaths followed when a mountain lion killed Bubba, one of the bucks. With hunting season, no deer was safe and hunters killed Babe. Joe identified him and even helped bring Babe onto the hunter's truck. All the happenings were too much for Joe, since he was a member of the herd. He couldn't go on in this environment. Mule deer migrate in the spring and before winter. When they return, some don't come back and that's what Hutto planned to do. That wasn't as easy as it sounded.

Mule deer are extremely intelligent with the largest brain of any deer in the world. They also have great challenges including winters with temperatures that can reach 35° below zero. Mountain lions, bears and wolves are predators. Don't forget the guys with weapons. Deer need protection. Otherwise they'll soon become extinct. The story of Joe and his herd first aired on PBS on April 16, 2014 in *Nature: Touching the Wild*. The video link is at pbs.org/wnet/nature/touching-the-wild-touching-the-wild/8679.

A deer more familiar to us is one with a white tail. The trail near my home is the Ellicott Creek Trailway, which I mentioned earlier. It's for hikers, non-motorized bikers, joggers, skateboarders, cross-country skiers, people pushing youngsters in buggies and those riding Segways. Not always on the trail but in the area are creatures: some fly and others just roam, including white tail deer. They're beautiful creatures and smart. That's why these deer are here – people aren't allowed to shoot them in this place near the University of Buffalo North Campus.

Years ago, deer had more places to inhabit, but then houses, condominiums and *business parks* were constructed. Those two words in italics are another annoying oxymoron. Deer were uprooted but manage to avoid the bullets of the hunters. During hunting season, they discover great hiding places. When it's over, they relax and continue living without worries. How do they know when the season began and when it's over?

Another huge animal that was almost hunted to extinction is the majestic American buffalo. In the middle of the nineteenth century, they numbered in the tens of millions. Some estimated that the number approached 60,000,000 and it was at least half that. The bison co-existed with the Native Americans. The latter hunted the buffalo for food and pelts, but did it environmentally. Towards the end of the century, the American government indiscriminately slaughtered the bison, almost wiping them out. This was done to reduce the food supply of the Native Americans, destroying them as well. It wasn't bad enough that the colonists took the land of those who were here before them; they signed treaties with the natives, which they soon broke, and forced them to live on reservations. Today, the buffalo population has recovered with about 20,000 – a far cry from what it was. At least they're not extinct.

Christopher Hogwood is a British musician, writer and conductor, associated with classical music. You may have heard of an animal with the same name. Before dealing with Chris, here are a few facts about pigs. The average life of a pig is about six

36

months, when they weigh about 250 pounds. This has to do with chops, bacon and ham. However, some can live six or seven years, but those are breeders. Because of their size and likelihood of crunching the young sows, many pigs won't be around more than a few months. Because they're so huge, very few question where they sleep. Sows probably won't find any enclosure that restricts them. More people get killed each year by pigs than by sharks. The reason should be obvious. If not, the clue is *land and water*.

Chris was only a baby when adopted by Sy Montgomery and her husband, Howard Mansfield, in Hancock, New Hampshire. He received his name because porcines love classical music and Chris was no exception. He grew slowly, only becoming as large as a cat. Eventually caretakers discovered what was holding him back and soon he grew bigger, as expected. This might have something to do with his voracious appetite. He wasn't allowed to eat meat – he probably wouldn't have hesitated at the chance – since he devoured everything else. Citrus and onions he left alone, though. He loved beer, with the local beer guy figuring that based on his weight, it would take two six-packs for him to get drunk. He may have tried weed.

This pig was great at leaving without being detected, although probably not as talented as an actor named Willie Sutton. Like other pigs that have great senses of smell, vision and hearing, Chris was smart. Even when he was smaller, if his enclosure was done with string, he could untie it and leave. Switching to bungee cords still didn't keep him in. He even figured out the next method of restraint, a complicated bolt. Chris must have used his lips and nose to free himself. One experiment with electric fencing to keep Chris from roaming failed miserably, so a harness was tried, a small one and then one larger. A twenty-foot tether tied to a strong tree gave him freedom and access to roam grass, shade and even a mud swallow. After a short time, Chris the digger made the area resemble a war zone after a bombing. He seemed to love it. Eventually he wound the tether around the tree in such a way that he could free himself from the harness. I told you he was clever.

When he left, he didn't travel far, only a quarter mile. In his journeys, Chris met many people whom he impressed, even residents who spotted him devouring lettuce – or just about anything else in their gardens. On one occasion, Howard looked

37

out the window and saw a jogger. Then he caught glimpse of a neighbor in a car. Then he saw Chris. Soon he and Sy ran outside. Fortunately, they never had to post bond for him.

It didn't take long for Chris to recognize his owners. He heard them approaching and was there to greet them. They thought that Chris didn't know where they lived – he must have known. Howard didn't want the pig to know because the latter could do a great deal of damage if he entered the home. He could also excavate with his snout – good for preparing a garden, but somewhat messy. Chris was loving, considerate and made friends easily, as you may have guessed. I'm sure he could sense which people were caring and those who weren't.

Chris's closeness to Montgomery and Mansfield, both writers, is accounted for by their love of nature and animals. Sy experiences this even when she travels, observing dolphins, tigers and great apes. In Australia on a Chicago Zoological Study trip, she caught sight of emus, who can travel 40 miles an hour. They have no problem demolishing fencing – I wonder from where they learned that. These four-foot tall flightless creatures can hurt visitors, yet, they got along well with Sy as they let her follow and observe them. For this experience and others, she was in a place she loved even though she missed her husband and Chris.

In another of her travels, Montgomery was in the area of the Sundarban's tigers. These beasts could easily kill a hunter, but she only had a few close calls as they all got along. Maybe the tigers knew she was a friend of the earth. The tiger protected the forest by scaring off the woodsmen so they refrained from cutting down trees. In turn, the shrubs and trees were protection against cyclones while their leaves and roots fed animals that people would take as food. The entire environment was all about balance.

Back home in New Hampshire, Sheriff Ed's most exciting days were capturing the runaway Chris. Other than that, there wasn't much crime in town and he may have been bored, but the porker changed matters. The sheriff spotted him and tied a rope around his neck to lead him home. Chris was reluctant to move so Ed decided to wait. Then Chris got moving, leading the sheriff down the road. Fortunately the leader was only moving at a jog – he was no sprinter. A passing driver asked Ed where he was going with Chris. His reply was, *He's going to do whatever he wants.*

Sy and Howard lived in a house with renters. Their place also had a few other animals, including egg producing hens and Tess, a border collie who had been mistreated by her owners. The dog was a bit shy, but fit in and reacted well to the environment. When a tenant departed, both Tess and Chris had to give their approval before the new renters moved in. Just the way the new people reacted to them made the decision easy for Sy and Howard. Lilla and her daughters, Jane and Kate, needed a home. Jane and Kate's love for Chris was all that was needed for the landlords' approval of the three. At that point, Lilla's anxiety disappeared since the family had found a great home.

Selinda came to the house with her two dogs, Numskull and Knucklehead – not their real names for security purposes. The three approved of the place and vice versa and soon Sy and Howard had new tenants. Selinda loved gardening and the landlords approved of the idea. She grew lettuce, zucchini, herbs, Swiss chard, beans and red peppers. There was other produce, but amazingly the porcine disposal unit kept away from it. Somehow Chris knew that he'd get clippings and benefits later. He was also the beneficiary of slop buckets from neighbors and restaurants. Donuts, stale baked goods and lasagna were some of the offerings. He wouldn't grow hungry. Soon, Chris tipped the scales at around 700 pounds. The heaviest pig on record, a Poland China hog named Big Bill, weighed in at 2500 pounds. Montgomery and her husband didn't want Chris to weigh more than their car, so they figured that 700 was a good number.

One day, friends of the couple, Bobbie and Jarvis, created a laminated sign and placed it on Sy and Howard's barn. A quote from St. Francis of Assisi said: *Not to hurt our humble brethren is our first duty to them, but to stop there is not enough. We have a higher mission: to be of service to them whenever they require it.*

Chris loved to eat. It satisfied him. The word, *satisfaction*, came from the French, *to make full*. It fit him but also expressed how Howard, Sy and many others felt about what the Chris did to their hearts. Another word beginning with the same letter is *success*. In Chris's case it applied to the fact that he escaped for more than fourteen years from the freezer. His life was a success in another way. He was written about in many newspapers. He was a star, giving comfort, happiness and joy to others, even those he never met. They returned this love to him. You can read more about Chris in Sy Montgomery's amusing book, *The Good Good Pig: The Extraordinary Life Of Christopher Hogwood.*

Charles Howard was born in the late 1870s in the eastern United States but when he was in his 20s, he moved to San Francisco with 21 cents to his name. Horses were replaced by cars and it wasn't long before Howard changed his few pennies into thousands of dollars, dealing with the automobile. He was living the life of luxury, even establishing the *Charles S. Howard Foundation* for children with tuberculosis and rheumatic fever.

In early May while he and his wife Fannie May were away from the ranch, his teenaged son, Frankie, went fishing with friends. On the way home with the lad driving an old truck of his dad, to avoid a huge boulder Frankie wound up flipping the vehicle over into the canyon. Stuck inside the truck, rescuers were too late to save the Howard child. Charles spent months with his grief, something he would never get over. One good thing that resulted was the *Frank R. Howard Memorial Hospital* opening in Willits in 1928.

When one mentions the word, *Sin City*, Las Vegas, New York and New Orleans come to mind. Another place not far from Howard's home is Tijuana, where anything goes. Charles made some trips there but stayed away from gambling, drinking and women. He instead went to the horse races. His friend, George Giannini owned some good racehorses but Howard wasn't that enthusiastic about them. Charles Doc Strub, a dentist who had played professional baseball, changed Howard's mind. In 1935, he had a few somewhat talented runners and hired Buster Millerick to train them. The horses Charles assembled weren't the greatest, but he bought them because no one else did. He wanted them to be winners so he figured he needed to replace his trainer with one who was the best.

Tom Smith talked only on occasion to people and probably saved his voice for the horses. Nonetheless, Smith was a legend, reportedly having chopped off his toe with an ax. It was said that the ax man took the severed foot part from his boot and commented, *My Toe.* Tom knew horses and *Cowboy Charlie* Irwin hired him as farrier, trainer and foreman. Irwin was in charge of a stable and ran a Wild West Show and apparently it was raucous.

Smith managed a horse named Oriley despite the fact that he was lame. Eventually Smith became the new trainer for Howard.

Charles had some horses and Smith to train them so they needed someone to ride them. You may know of the horrible lives of those who work at Amazon warehouses today – slave labor, minimal pay with no benefits under horrible working conditions – but jockeys' lives in the early twentieth century weren't any better, maybe worse. Their pay was low except for the very best ones and all jockeys had to be in top shape. When riding, they didn't sit on the horse, instead being raised in the air with their feet in the stirrups. Falling off the horse may not have been that common, but many were tossed off the animals, resulting in broken bones and cracked skulls, or worse. Horses weighing upwards of half a ton didn't make life easier on the track. Jockeys had no insurance so admittance to the hospital could only be done if fellow riders chipped in. They had to weigh from 80 to 120 pounds to make the grade requiring them to almost join the anorexia nervosa society – they ate little and purged. This led to dehydration, hunger, weakness and some bizarre ways of meeting that weight limit. It's not surprising that many riders hung themselves or used guns to commit suicide.

Johnny Pollard was from a family that if you included his parents, John and Edith, had enough for a baseball team. He was a scrappy boxer who read as many books as he could. In school, he had no respect for his teachers, achieved bad grades but was happy pulling pranks. Becoming a jockey in his teens, a decade later, he was one of the worst at it. Because of the color of his hair, many called him *Red*. He loved riding but it was a rough life for him; he was often hungry, desperate for money. He was, according to his sister Edie, *happy as heck*. Possessing a skill to handle the horses, the animals performed for him, especially the rogues. Not making much money, nevertheless he sent cash back to his parents and also gave to others who needed a lift. He didn't ask to be repaid.

During one workout, Red was hit by a rock or some hunk of dirt dug up by another horse working out. That incident resulted in the permanent loss of sight in his right eye. This secret was kept from people in the business because otherwise, he really wouldn't be hired to ride the ponies. In August 1936, Johnny was riding in the car of an agent named Yummy when the car hit an object, totaling the vehicle. They wound up at a racetrack in Detroit. It was here that the union of Howard, Smith and Pollard took place.

Seabiscuit was a horse that Smith thought had potential. He was with the Howard crew when Red joined them. Seabiscuit slept a great deal and supplemented his meals with any extras available. He had a mind of his own and couldn't be pushed. When he wanted to, he could really run, though. Because of his habits, Smith figured the horse needed company. Whiskers the goat didn't fare well as Smith noticed Seabiscuit shaking his head with Whiskers in his mouth. Pumpkin, another horse, a dog named Pocatell, and Jo Jo, a spider monkey were the companions that Seabiscuit accepted.

The horse learned and was quite intelligent, catching on quickly. Smith spoke to him and Seabiscuit listened. Red did the same with him and felt that with training, he had great potential. In a stakes race in Detroit, Myrtlewood, the best filly in the country, was out front but Seabiscuit was running well. Suddenly he dropped back. When the horse resumed his attempt to catch up, he wound up in fourth place only four lengths behind Myrtlewood. Red found that Seabiscuit possessed courage and real speed. Pollard thought that he could have a champion.

In September the Governor's Handicap was a big race in Detroit. Seabiscuit had long odds but was close behind Biography. When Pollard saw a hole, he moved his horse into the lead. Professor Paul and Azucar were right behind but Pollard's horse won the race. At the Santa Anita Handicap, Seabiscuit was out in front but Pollard forgot about the opposition, Rosemont. His partial blindness played a part. At the wire, the two horses were tied. The photo at the finish line would determine the winner. Howard passed out the champagne for everyone, but Rosemont won the event.

The 1930s were a difficult time for many Americans suffering because of the Depression. Radio filled the void as did horse racing. When Seabiscuit raced, the number of listeners tuning in numbered 40 million. At the $15,000 San Juan Capistrano, 45,000 fans crowded into the stands to see this magnificent horse run. At the beginning of the race, Special Agent moved out in the lead with Seabiscuit behind him. By the end of the race, Pollard and the wonder horse cruised to a win by a huge margin.

Howard welcomed the press while Pollard and Smith weren't that friendly to the media. The pair managed all kinds of tricks to confuse those ink-stained wretches. Grog became a part of the Howard contingent, looking quite a bit like Seabiscuit. Many times Grog was doing some training while the press thought it was Seabiscuit. The media had no idea which horse they were looking at when he ran. Smith and Pollard were having a great time.

Seabiscuit could run but was slowed down by injuries, which affected many thoroughbreds. Heavy rains resulting in muddy footing, weren't to his liking either. This led to his being scratched from races. This kept him out of the San Carlos Handicap on February 20, 1938, but Pollard was still set to ride Fair Knightess, who did well in the mud. Nevertheless, Red should have called in sick. The amount of danger on the track increased as the number of horses in the event grew larger. On that day, the forelegs of Pollard's horse were kicked out from under her. The jockey went down and Fair Knightess wound up on top of him. Besides having his chest crushed, Red had other injuries and was barely conscious when he was rushed to *St. Luke's Hospital* in Pasadena. With time, Pollard healed but doctors offered that he wouldn't ride for a year or more.

In May 1938, Red was riding on Fair Knightess at Belmont Park in New York. Miraculously, both had recovered. At the Handspring Handicap, the jockey and his horse fired out of the gate to a commanding lead and no one could catch them. They were easy victors. It looked like Pollard was ready. It was said that he wouldn't mount a horse for a year but he had recovered from his injuries in three months. The next month as a favor to his friend Bert Blume, he agreed to work out Modern Youth. The horse was soon out of control and smashed into a barn, seriously injuring Johnny.

While Red was slowly recovering, George Woolf did a fine job substituting and winning with Seabiscuit. Despite these victories, the thoroughbred got no respect from the eastern racing establishment. Their champion was War Admiral with whom Howard tried to set up a race. It didn't work out until November 1, 1938 at the Pimlico Special. Woolf rode Biscuit, but Pollard gave him plenty of advice. Seabiscuit wasn't given a chance of winning, as War Admiral was favored by every single *Daily Racing Form* handicapper and 95% of the writers. Over 40,000 fans crowded the racetrack for one of the America's most historic racing events. They weren't disappointed – unless they favored the Admiral. Woolf finished in first place, four lengths in front of his opponent.

Pollard was ecstatic as were Howard, Smith and Woolf. Red would heal and ride Seabiscuit again, winning at Santa Anita – something that Howard waited long for. Throughout their time together both Red and his horse had succumbed to numerous injuries, but had never given up. Seabiscuit had a huge following at race arenas as well as on the radio. He broke one record after another and then followed it up with another record-breaking outing. He may have been the greatest thoroughbred of all time.

In 2003, the movie, *Seabiscuit* starring Elizabeth Banks, Jeff Bridges and Tobey Maguire hit the silver screen. It was nominated for an Academy Award as best picture. I recommend it as well as the book by Lauren Hillenbrand, *Seabiscuit: An American Legend*. It's a great story of hope, love and dedication, which is filled with information about the sport, having a few laughs, too.

Zebras are members of the horse family, the African kind. Scientific research has shown that they are black with the white parts being added on. The reason for this combination is to hide and confuse their predators, such as hyenas and lions. It's great camouflage and also a way for their friends and family to recognize them, especially since each zebra has distinctive color patterns. In the 1979 movie, *The Electric Horseman*, if Robert Redford came into town riding on a zebra wearing a matching suit, people would have been more surprised by the animal he was riding. You'd also have to ask why he was wearing a suit.

The three species of the animal are the mountain zebra, Grévy's zebra and the plains zebra, with the first two being endangered. The plains or Burchell's zebras are the most common. The average lifespan of a zebra is about 25 years although some residing in zoos have lived to be 40. They aren't solitary but rather social animals that spend time in herds. Grazing together, primarily on grass, they groom one another.

John Byers and his wife Karen spent a few months thoroughly observing and studying pronghorn in the *National Bison Range* of western Montana. Naturally they encountered other animals but concentrated on the antelope. With a huge stride length, this creature can outrun just about any other animal and at the same time not tire. Moving at 60 miles an hour, it can go from one end of a football field to the other in less than four seconds. Do the math and if you want to be more exact, use three and a half seconds in your calculation for the time.

To study these swift runners, the Byers used tags on their ears and had others on the team, who utilized binoculars. Shortly after giving birth, mothers seemed to be moving around reminiscent of a Chinese fire drill. This was done for a few reasons: to keep predators away from the fawns and to rummage for food. They stayed in an area close to the newborns. When a coyote killed the offspring, the parent behaved as though the fawn were still alive. They did this for a couple days even if only some part of the animal remained. I won't go into specifics because it's gross and disgusting, but mothers can tell if a fawn has some infection. She can then produce antibodies to overcome the health problem and pass them on to the young.

As far as who reigned as boss, the earlier a pronghorn was born into a family, the more dominant she was. The same applied to the male, but he dominated over any female. Those at the top also were blessed with reclining privileges – they could lie down before the lesser of the group. As far as an advantage to this order, Byers found that there wasn't much. In fact, in general those at the bottom lived longer than those who dominated them. Unfortunately, the lowliest were on the outside and more easily available to predators.

The animals grow fast – two and a half pounds in five days. So besides the tags, the observers used this information to determine who was who as well as giving names to the pronghorn based on physical traits. At times this same sprouting led to identification confusion. The Byers expedition had daylight from about five a.m. until ten p.m. in the summer, making for long days. In other times of the year, the day was much shorter and colder too.

To survive the winter, pronghorn need plenty of stored fat. Males have less time to store the energy as they spend a great deal of time chasing the females, who can garner the needed nutrients. As a result, the male only survives about eight years while the female pronghorn manages to last twice that. Winters in Montana are brutal.

John couldn't help but observe bison in the reserve. Weighing about half a ton – the females weren't as big – this animal was massive, powerful and fast. One photographer with a *disposable* camera wanted a closer picture of the animal. She was soon pursued by the buffalo – disposable was the right word here – and was fortunate to suffer some bruises and some broken ribs. She was also rewarded with a citation from a Range officer. She should have known better. Originally, roundup chutes for bison were made of wood. That was until one buffalo moved through the three by twelve plank and left a huge hole. From then on, steel was used.

But getting back to pronghorn, maybe they are jocks, but can they pass the entrance exam? From what I've written, you can see that they're smart and athletic but come on; they certainly won't get a diploma or even be on the Rams taxi squad. Nonetheless, they're amazing animals. John A. Byers chronicled the project in his book, *Built For Speed: A Year In The Life Of Pronghorn.*

In the mid 1970s I bought my first house in Somers, a town in New York State about 45 miles north of New York City. I soon discovered it was in horse country. East of there is more of the same in Connecticut. Kentucky and Virginia are known for raising thoroughbreds. Horseracing is the sport of kings, most likely because it seems to be run by people with money: owners and breeders. The dollars stay within a handful of families and those less affluent have a tough time entering the pack. Of course, there are exceptions, including Christopher Chenery. As a young boy, he and his brothers went barefoot from early spring until fall, but not by choice. His best present at Christmas was a tangerine, but they were a close family and Chris loved horses.

Chenery set out to rise out of poverty and succeeded as very few had done, becoming the head of a few utility companies. He was wealthy but then used the money for his love: horses. Buying large acreage and horses to go with it, he also hired the best people he could to make the ponies champions: breeders, jockeys and trainers.

Just as the dollars stay with a few chosen relatives, the outstanding horses are also related. The best way to form champion racers is by judicious breeding. When a great thoroughbred mare gets together with a male horse that won the Triple Crown, the result should be a winner. That's why first place finishers seem to have ancestors who achieved the same honor. This has been going on for years.

The foal was born just after midnight on March 31, 1970 in horse country just north of Richmond, Virginia. His mother was a broodmare by the name of Somethingroyal, from the line of Princequillo and Imperatrice. Bold Ruler was the colt's father, winner of the 1957 Preakness Stakes, member of the Racing Hall of Fame and the leading sire in North America in the years 1963-1969 and 1973. Both parents were from great stock. The union could only produce another winner. At the time, manager Howard Gentry uttered, *There is a whooper.*

Some of the suggested names for the red colt were Scepter, Royal Line, Games of Chance and Deo Volente. The daughter of Chris Chenery, Mrs. Penny Tweedy, suggested the last two. Miss Elizabeth Ham had been a secretary of diplomat Norman Davis and came up with Secretariat, which became the colt's name. As he grew, many thought he would be a champion. In his first race at Aquaduct, Paul Feliciano rode him, but finished fourth, after a slow beginning and much bumping. Towards the end of the run, the red horse picked up speed and impressed both Penny and trainer Lucien Laurin.

Secretariat brought home $480 in that first try, but won the second race, winning ten times as much. All the jockeys loved the horse. Lucien wanted Ron Turcotte to ride the horse the next race day but Turcotte was recovering from a horrible accident while riding Overproof, who perished from a heart attack on the track. Ron was out of action for almost a month. For the rest of 1972, Secretariat finished in first place eight times in nine races, being disqualified for some bumping once. Even that was a questionable call. He was some thoroughbred, destined for great things. There were plans for him winning the Kentucky Derby and then capturing the Triple Crown.

47

Chris Chenery had been hospitalized and then died in January 1973. Penny took over the business since her siblings didn't want it. Her experience with horses was limited but she knew enough people to succeed. One big problem had to do with a huge estate tax liability. One remedy was to sell off some of the prize horses, but the executive committee thought that wasn't wise. The alternative chosen was to syndicate Secretariat. For $190,000, interested parties could have the chance to mate their mares with the red horse. At the same time a coup was brewing in Ireland to buy the colt for six to seven million dollars. Enough people signed on to the syndicate so that didn't happen.

In 1973, Secretariat and the crew moved north to New York where the horse would get ready for the Derby. The first race on March 17 in the Bay Shore was a tough challenge as the other horses boxed him in. Somehow Turcotte, but mostly the colt, burst out of the pack to win the race by over four lengths. He won again and the final tune up was at the Wood Memorial on April 21. Shortly before that day, Secretariat had an abscess on his lip, which didn't seem that big an issue. Sham, another Derby hopeful was entered in the Wood as was Angle Light, one of the ponies that Laurin trained. On race day, the red horse was not himself and Ron saw that as he rode him. Turcotte took it easy and Secretariat finished in third, disappointing many fans, especially those in the syndicate. Angle Light finished first beating Sham as his rider, Laffit Pincay, Jr., was looking behind him for the red horse.

The derby was next and Turcotte, Tweedy and Laurin still believed in the horse, but there was some doubt. When Turcotte found out about the abscess, it all made sense about the horse's behavior at the Wood Memorial and he was somewhat assured. At the start of the race on Derby day, the red horse was behind but as in so many races he passed one horse after the other, eventually beating Sham. He set a record that day and was just amazing. He repeated that at the Preakness in Maryland but the timekeepers said that no record was broken. Two other sources confirmed that he set another record, but the initial judgment stood.

Finally the third leg of the Triple Crown came at Belmont in New York. This race was different. Secretariat came out of the gates running. He did it by himself as Turcotte let him fly. In most races, Ron did the same thing with the horse moving at his own pace. At times Turcotte talked and encouraged him to move faster. As the colt blazed, people thought Ron was having the horse run way too fast, but Turcotte wasn't really in charge. Secretariat set another record, winning by 31 lengths. This may have been the best thoroughbred of all time. The other entrants in the race, including Sham, were tired but not Penny's boy.

Besides his athletic prowess, Secretariat was very intelligent. One day he grabbed the rake and started cleaning up. Another time, sports writer William Nack was near when the colt grabbed his notebook. *Give the man his notebook back*, said groom Eddie Sweat. Secretariat dropped it. Before race day, photographers came around and the colt cooperated, pricking up his ears in approval, knowledgeable of what was going on. He could also get as on edge as Laurin. On racing day, his allotment of oats was reduced, the straw in his stall wasn't the same as on other days and Secretariat knew he'd be racing. When the Kentucky Derby winner went to chew on some grass outside the paddock, Billy Silver, a stable pony who loved the horse, wanted to join him there. Billy Silver knew what a champion Secretariat was. Long before he was born, Bold Ruler's father, Nasrullah, died of suffocation. When that happened, Bold Ruler was uncontrollable. He never nickered until that day, so upset was he that one of his parents had perished.

You can read much more about the great horse in the book by William Nack, *Secretariat*. A few years before, Nack wrote *Big Red Of Meadow Stable: Secretariat, The Making Of A Champion*. The movie *Secretariat* starring Diane Lane and John Malkovich hit the silver screen in 2010.

The Royal Family has their share of animals, especially dogs and horses. The Queen loves her corgies – pampered, of course and enough for a soccer team. Prince William and Princess Catherine prefer cocker spaniels. As the corgies die off, they're not replaced. The chefs actually cook for the dogs with more consideration than given the meals of visiting heads of state. Too often, the animals, whose legs are too short, are released into the kitchen, which annoys the cooks. In one way, these dogs are trained. They can't start eating until the queen gives the go ahead. Unfortunately, when waste is emitted, these corgis could care less where it is deposited. This doesn't thrill staff members since they have to do the cleanup.

According to the October 16, 2014 episode of the CBC program the *Doc Zone: Royals & Animals: Till Death Do Us Part, The Queen's private passions follow this order*, says former royal butler Paul Burrell, *horses, dogs, husband and kids*. Sorry, children! Prince Philip famously said of Princess Anne: *If it doesn't fart or eat hay, she isn't interested.*

Queen Elizabeth is also a horse person and not averse to placing a bet on the latter from time to time. Her mom was even more addicted to gambling on the ponies, amassing huge losses. She probably didn't check the racing news that often. Queen Mom should have gone to the casino rather than the track. I wonder if the household servants saw smaller paychecks because of her habit. Elizabeth II was blessed to meet an outstanding horse handler, and I'll return to the Royal Family soon.

Born in Salinas, California, Monty Roberts was riding at the age of two and really didn't have a childhood. He followed in the footsteps of his father, whose life evolved around the ponies. He differed from his father in one horse matter: Marvin believed in the old school of breaking a horse while Monty took the more gentle approach. He talked in a low voice to the animal and understood its body language. Monty also used it. He gave his work the name *join-up*. It didn't matter if the horse was wild or not. He also began his handling as a teenager and spent days observing wild horses. His methods were practiced millennia ago when soldier and writer Xenophon preached the kinder way in ancient Greece. More recently in the nineteenth century, John Solomon Rarey followed what Xenophon advocated. Native Americans also used the compassionate approach where man and horse were equals and whipping was not only unnecessary, but also counterproductive. It's no surprise that Roberts had the same feeling since he was part Cherokee.

As cruel as many trainers and owners are, it's much worse when the animals are sent to war. They would run away if they knew what was in store for them. Over three millennia ago, in a battle between the Hittites and Egyptians, 7,000 horses were used. In 1815, the Battle of Waterloo was more brutal with the French and British employing 30,000 horses. Of the 1.5 million animals of the species used in World War I, a third of them died, many from hunger and parasites. Commerce in peacetime wasn't kind to the ponies either.

Monty is colorblind, only seeing black, white and gray. For him that isn't a handicap, since he is blessed with better perception in his faculties. Had he not been deprived of appreciating the changing colors of autumn, he may never have achieved all he has done with horses. Monty can see at night better or just as well as those with night vision goggles. He has great depth perception, able to see subtle shadings and the density of pigments. He had another challenge when he was told his riding days were over after lower back surgery in 1981. The surgeons had it wrong. After hospitals, therapy, and months of healing, Roberts said, *I can walk fine, and I can ride*. Monty is one tough individual, a great teacher and possessor of a great work ethic.

Referring to Monty at a demonstration one day in December 1995, Dr. William O. Reed of the North American track veterinarians said:

> *I thought it was the greatest communication between man and animal I had ever seen. Monty Roberts is definitely a pioneer. In the past, horse breaking has been man against horse, checking his will, dominating him. Monty does something quite different.*

From the novel, *My Friend Flicka* by Mary O'Hara, come these thoughts from the rancher:

> *Remember, a horse can tell you a lot of things, if you watch, and expect it to be sensible and intelligent. Pay attention to all the little signs – the way it moves its body, the ears, the eyes, the little whinnies – that's its way of talking. She'll talk to you, and it's for you to understand her. You learn her language, and she'll learn yours – never forget that 'they can understand everything you say to them.'*

It's time to change our feeling about Doctor Doolittle. St. Francis of Assisi is the patron saint of animals and the environment. He didn't limit his communications to horses alone. Roberts' home has a statue of the great man, who was never ordained a Catholic priest.

Besides his other life events, Monty spent time in a cell with a murderer who was meant to kill him, all because of his overseer, Hastings Harcourt. The latter was about to sell all the horses and his farm, *Flag Is Up Farms*, where Monty lived with his family. Harcourt asked Monty to shoot some of the animals, which Roberts refused to do. It was a tough time for the Roberts' family as their lives were in grave danger. The result was handed over to court and Monty prevailed. He also talked the guy in the cell down.

Monty participates in many horse events. On one occasion, he decided to enter Johnny Tivio in both the reined cow horse division and cutting division. An old friend, Lester Sterling, thought it was a bad idea, but Roberts went ahead anyway. He and Johnny Tivio won both events. Before that day, no one had done this and it hasn't been tried since. Roberts managed to come out on top with his horses many more times. He was a great trainer and breeder and his method worked. In his own words,

> *The 'crazy horse' is almost never born, but made. And it pains me to hear the term. If we could somehow see for ourselves all the events in a horse's life that together account for his malicious behavior, we would be astonished. Some horses will take so much, then finally take no more.*

Roberts' old friend Crawford Hall fell off a horse in 1974, breaking his neck. After hospital time he became a quadriplegic, given another three to five years to live. His friends were more encouraging and Crawford wasn't giving up, soon mastering moving around in his wheelchair. Monty gave him a job at *Flag Is Up Farms* and after a year he managed the training operation. Crawford said, *The horses themselves were therapeutic.* In the early 1990s, Hall had been on the farm for over two decades. He has been inspirational for what he accomplished as hospitals and therapists have a video of him for others facing similar challenges.

Crawford was always a prankster and his accident didn't change that. One involved Corky Parker, whose birthday was approaching. He was informed of the visit by an Arab sheik, who was looking for a major horse deal. Many of the staff were involved as was a bogus stretch limousine. Farm associate Satish Seemat donned the robes of the *sheik* and Corky bought into it. The guys had a good laugh. Once, a young rider at the farm worried that a horse would run away, Hall said, *How can he do that? You have the Atlantic on your right and the Pacific on your left. Where's he going to do?*

Getting back to the queen, hearing about Roberts also gave me insight into the royals. For the Queen, Monty did many demonstrations to people in England on the gentle approach after she heard of his magic with horses. I have to thank the CBC who enlightened me on that family and Roberts. The *Doc Zone* episode is worth watching again. Without Queen Elizabeth, Monty may not have written his book, *The Man Who Listens To Horses: The Story Of A Real-life Horse Whisperer*. The 1998 movie, *The Horse Whisperer*, starring Sam Neill, Kristin Scott Thomas and Robert Redford, who also directed it, is based on Roberts' life. The novel of the same name is by Nicholas Evans. The BBC also did a documentary on him in 1997, *Monty Roberts: The Real Horse Whisperer*.

Many members of the Royal Family love animals so much that they hunt them, and eat them. At least once, a family cat was accidentally shot – oops! Bagging some game, royal hunters have it cooked by the chefs, then bragging to the guests that he killed what they were about to eat. I don't think too many women went in for the sport, certainly not Princess Diana, who loved animals but not shooting at them. At one time there was a royal zoo, but it seems to be toned down now. In a way, the zoo still exists but I think to be fair, the captive animals should be armed to fire back.

The song, "Stewball" is found on the 1964 album of Peter, Paul & Mary, *In the Wind*. I had a difficult time choosing a chapter title because there are so many good songs about horses, domesticated or wild.

5. Octopus's garden

I'm not a big fan of television since there's so much junk there. In the *Wasteland Speech* of May 9, 1961, Federal Communications Commissioner chairman, Newton N. Minow, called commercial television a *vast wasteland*. I wonder how he feels today. At that time Newton put out a call for something better for the public. Someone listened, but not enough people. Thankfully, there are some great programs on public television (*PBS*) and the *Canadian Broadcasting Corporation* (CBC). I'm fortunate to have two Canadian stations from Toronto in my cable list as well as a pair of the former: the normal PBS offering and the *World Channel*. *The Nature of Things* with David Suzuki is on the CBC most Thursday nights and on the weekend. *Nature* and *Nova* are both on PBS.

An episode of *The Nature of Things* featured some experiments with octopi, so let's call the creature in the first case, Willie. It began with placing him – or maybe it was a she – in a Plexiglas enclosure with a small hole to exit. The aperture was just large enough for Willie to get out, dependent on the size of his head. She moved one arm through the hole, followed slowly by another until all the arms were through the opening. Willie then made his mantle as small as possible and departed the box, which seemed easy. Next, a smaller opening was introduced, and Willie tried one arm but then stopped his efforts, knowing he was stuck in the box. A few other octopi went through the test with the same results.

Another test involved an enclosure with two holes – one too small for exiting – and a complicated system of plastic tubes and openings heading in many directions. Once the creature left the enclosure, he would get through but he did it slowly. To start he picked the larger opening and then cautiously used the same method with his arms that he did earlier. He found freedom from the maze. Using the same setup for a second try, he was home free in a flash.

The next trial involved two octopi, a teacher and a student. There were two Plexiglas boxes having three lids with a crab inside. One cover was easily removed while the other two required twisting. The teacher knew how to get his food from one box; with the other octopus watching, he demonstrated how to do it. The student had his food just by watching his elder. Then a barrier was put between the two octopi so the learner was on his own. It didn't matter as the crab was soon captured.

An octopus is a *Cephalopod*, which also includes squids, nautili and cuttlefish. Despite their scary appearance, octopi are blessed with skin of brilliant color. They can change size, shape and their color to blend in with their environment, avoiding predators. They emit a dark liquid having the shape of an octopus, again enabling escape. Each has a beak that you should avoid unless you don't mind razors, and they're as tall as a human. That is some marine monster, whose scientific name is *Octopus vulgaris*. *Cephalopods* range in size from the blue-ringed octopus – it may be small, but it's deadly – to the huge aggressive Humboldt squid. The latter puts on quite a light show, but I think it's a cannibal.

An octopus can move along in a straight path while rotating its body. What other beings can do that? Also, its eight tentacles are part of a complicated nervous system. They seem to be independent of each other. Octopi slither and move about rotating their bodies while never having to ask for directions.

Willie has cousins in squids, which seem to fly. Doing so, they save energy. High-speed photography seemed to confirm this. Squid use the same mechanisms whether they move through the water or through the air. Marine biologist, Ronald O'Dor, from Dalhousie University in Halifax, would find dead shortfin squid in the morning around the pool, but not in it. Most likely they weren't on their way for a snack, so it seems one of their flying missions went bad. The solution was a simple one: lower the water level. A few other marine biologists confirmed the above dealings with those squid movements, including Julia Stewart from Hopkins Marine Station of Stanford University. Some researchers determined that this speed was five times as fast as that under water. There's more about the octopus and squid in *Encountering Sea Monsters*, the *Nature* special, which first aired in December 2005.

Leatherback sea turtles were around in some form over one hundred million years ago. They're amazing creatures as they travel a thousand miles to lay their eggs. Scientists monitored one who traveled twelve thousand miles in less than two years. One of those places you can see them is near Trinidad, an island north of the coast of South America. They find a place on the beaches and lay their eggs – a few times each year – around a hundred at a time. They clear a spot, emit the eggs and then hide them under a warm layer of sand. In a few weeks, tiny little creatures break out of their shells. They head out into the ocean but unfortunately only one or two out of a thousand make it into adulthood. The mother leaves but then returns to the same place every year, an amazing feat.

Also called the lute turtle, there are no bigger turtles and it's the fourth heaviest reptile. It can be differentiated from other turtles because it doesn't have a hard shell. Lute turtles are among marine animals that dive the deepest, having been recorded at a depth of 4,200 feet. Although their normal speed in miles per hour is in the single digits, the Guinness Book of Records listed them as reaching almost 22 mph. The life span of a leatherback is about 30 years, although it's been speculated that they can live for 50 years.

Another not so great sea creature is the lionfish. Found primarily in the Pacific and Indian Oceans, the lionfish is a beautiful creature, but venomous despite its red, white and black coloration. Also known as pterois, it recently arrived in the Caribbean and has started to rapidly multiply. It survives in warm waters. Here it is a menace as it eats other species that are necessary for balance in the sea. It doesn't do any good for the coral, either. The lionfish made its way into the Caribbean when some individual dumped a pet lionfish into a stream or lake and it made its way into the ocean. They can be found in the warm waters of the Atlantic from the United States all the way down the coast of South America.

This invasive species has few predators while being a vicious predator itself. As scientist Carl Safina discovered, there aren't many ways to capture them. One way is with two small nets, one on top of the other, thus trapping them. It's a long process though. Another is with a spear type devise. This method is tedious as well. The good news is that lionfish have become a culinary delicacy. In the Bahamas, people may have found a solution to this overabundance of the creature: fishing derbies. Though lionfish in the Caribbean number in the millions, these contests seem to be lowering the population. People are fighting back, alleviating a huge problem and then settling down to a lionfish dinner. It tastes just like chicken.

As the summer of 2014 was winding down, I turned over the calendar for September. The creature featured for that month is a pufferfish. If you've tasted it, consider yourself fortunate. If not prepared correctly by the chef, it might be your last meal. The only vertebrate more poisonous is the golden poison frog. People still order that fish from the menu, since it's a delicacy. Then again, some individuals climb Mt. Everest, skydive, go bungee jumping, climb walls of ice, or just plain vertical rocks. It's all done as a sense of adventure. Could I have a piece of broiled salmon?

I wonder if poached piranha is another delicacy delight or a dangerous dinner entrée. You might think that fish is a cannibal, but actually it's nothing more than a predator, like so many other animals – two legged ones with rifles, too. Besides the pufferfish, there are things you should stay away from since you may get sick or worse if you eat them. I'm not talking only about badly prepared seafood. The list of poisonous plants is really long, including apple seeds, cassava, poinsettia, rhubarb leaves, nutmeg, mountain laurel, daffodils and both holly and ivy. In many cases, cooking may render them harmless and some will affect only humans or only some animals. Some birds will indulge in these plants and be fine while some plants are loaded with poison to keep certain animals away. You may not want to search the Internet for this list since you'll wind up with a very limited diet.

In 1961, Harry Goodridge of Rockport, Maine, saw a seal pup struggling in the ocean, so he came to its aid. His job was to feed and nurture it. Two years before he had taken in a pup but it died shortly after being rescued. This time Harry figured the young seal, who was only a few days old, needed really rich milk to survive. He concocted a blend with eggs and cream for Andre. Somehow that still wasn't good enough so he simulated a feeding method similar to a mother seal. That was a success and Andre grew as he looked on Goodridge as his parent.

The master taught the seal some tricks and soon Andre entertained tourists. Harry always felt that Andre should be free to leave whenever he felt like doing so, even if the boss never saw him again. Andre's home was a floating enclosure, which was always open for him so could move out into the ocean. There was always the danger of sharks but the seal handled himself well in avoiding them. Andre left, but always returned. Harry and Andre had formed a bond.

A serious problem arose with the coming of winter. Goodridge figured that the seal would have difficulty when the water froze. The solution was to take him to the *New England Aquarium* for those months. The trip there wasn't something Andre cared for so Harry let him swim home. With the journey distance of over 150 miles, Rockport residents were concerned, especially the Goodridge family. Harry pretended he wasn't worried, but deep inside he was. When Andre sauntered into Penobscot Bay, the town felt great relief. To make the long trip indicated how smart he was. He repeated this feat for over 20 years, making him the honorary harbormaster.

In the 1980s, Andre couldn't continue to do some of the tricks he had done for audiences. Harry realized he was becoming blind. The seal still found his way home on his yearly trips. One day in July 1986, he didn't return. He was found dead and was buried in a plot and a few years later his trainer would join him when he died. In 1978, a statue was dedicated to Andre in the harbor that Harry himself unveiled. *The Seal Who Came Home*, which premiered on Wednesday, July 2, 2014, was part of the *My Wild Affair* series on PBS.

Wildlife centers exist all over the world. Their goal is rescue, rehabilitation and reintroduction into the wild. One center is the *Monterey Bay Aquarium* on the coast of California. Recently they had a visitor to whom they assigned the name Otter 501. This may have been done for a reason. There was great need to keep the caretaker from getting too close to the otter, and vice versa. More likely it was the 501st effort to help an otter. The workers wore black clothes and headgear similar to what the police wore at the 1968 Democratic Convention, but they were much more considerate. The first step was to provide nutrients for the baby otter, which was done. He grew, and after a while, a matriarch was found. Toola cared for the young ones and was needed to teach Otter 501 the things so she could be released.

It took a few days before Toola and Otter 501 got along. After five days it appeared that the baby otter had found a mother.

From the latter, Otter 501 would get the knowledge so that she would be ready to be released into the wild, including being a master diver. That's how otters find food, and they need vast amounts of it to survive. It appeared that Otter 501 was finally ready to make it on her own. However, on checking on the otter, staff noticed she still wasn't able to make it, so they brought her back for a few more days. With the next release, Otter 501 did manage to fit into her wild environment. Soon, caretakers found her with one of her own young.

"Octopus's Garden" is from the Beatles' 1969 album, *Abbey Road*. Written and sung by Richard Starkey – we known him by the name of Ringo Starr – it was the final song released by the group that had him doing the lead vocal.

6. Hummingbird

There are numerous songs about flying creatures. The title above represents one of my favorite songs by Seals and Crofts. It's from their 1972 album, *Summer Breeze*, which was their fourth. The record was a breakthrough for them and hit number seven on the billboard chart. "Hummingbird" reached number six on the pop chart.

Irene grew up in Brooklyn and Queens and was an only child. At school in the former, she didn't fit in. She didn't have too many friends but had a parrot as pet at the age of four. She doesn't remember his or her name but recalls the appellations for others: Greeny, Bluey and two named Charlie Bird. Those last two couldn't play the saxophone. As far as I know, the only animals that are musicians are the Muppets. In high school Irene was a nerd, finishing near the top. She excelled in French and history and loved chemistry. Before graduation, she considered Cornell, then Radcliffe, but applied to the Massachusetts Institute of Technology and was accepted.

She did well and before graduating met David Pepperberg, who was a few years ahead of her at the school. Graduate school for her was Harvard and the pair dated. Then they married, moving into a small studio apartment in Cambridge. In November 1973, their home burned down and John Dowling, who was David's advisor, took them into his home. The next year *Nature* made its debut on PBS. After seeing an episode, Irene was captivated by animals and their communication with humans. This may have been the initiative to leave the chemistry agenda and become involved with animal behavior.

She decided on birds rather than chimpanzees because it seemed easier and she had had parrots for pets so she already knew how to talk to them. Her choice was the African Grey Parrot, which went back four thousand years. Egyptians, Greeks and Romans raised them as pets as did King Henry VIII. They were gorgeous creatures, gray with white around the eyes and a red tail. They also were known for the bonds they made with their masters.

In the beginning of January 1977, David and Irene moved to West Lafayette, Indiana. Six months later they went to the pet store, *Noah's Ark*, and picked out a Grey, and named him Alex. The bird with the forgotten name weighed about an ounce, but the Grey came in at almost a pound and was ten inches tall. The ride back home was three hours and Alex didn't seem happy about it. As a result, it took him sometime to bond with Irene. They were times when Irene wrote a journal entry saying that Alex was grumpy, stupid, crazy, dumb, grouchy and impossible.

Alex was no dumb bird, though. He was trained to identify a key that was colored silver, but also recognized a red one. Psychologists refer to what Alex had done as *transfer*. When people spoke, he learned. Hearing *no* resulted in his reply of *nuh*. It meant *no, I don't want to* and Alex soon replaced the *nuh* with *no*. He really knew what the word meant and was capable of identifying shapes, sizes and colors. Parrots chew things, such as index cards, telephone cables, important documents – like a grant proposal – and just about anything else. All Greys do. Alex loved playing with corks. He was given one and destroyed most of it and asked for another. Irene mentioned that he had a cork, what was left of it. Alex replied, *no*, meaning he wanted another. Soon he replied, *cork*, proving he was no bird brain.

When his owner saw the devastated grant proposal, she admonished him. He responded, *I'm sorry . . . I'm sorry*. A short time before Alex's document destruction, Irene said those words and he picked up on it. This African Grey could be described as haughty, precocious, social as well as intelligent. One day, Kathy Davidson brought Alex into the washroom and the African Grey saw himself in a mirror. He asked, *What's that?* Davidson replied, *That's you. You're a parrot.* Alex said, *What color?* Her reply of *gray* was how he learned that color.

Alex knew what bananas, cherries and grapes were. I'm not sure which was his favorite. When given an apple, he replied *Banerry . . . I want bannery.* What he had done was combine banana and cherry to come up with his response. Another time at the vets' he asked an accountant on the scene if she wanted a nut, which she refused. He added, *You want corn?* Her reply was *No thank you, Alex, I don't want corn.* This banter went on until the bird asked, *Well, what do you want?*

Irene and David drifted apart and on the Sunday after Thanksgiving, she and the Grey were on their way to O'Hare

Airport for a flight to Tucson, where she had a job at the University of Arizona. Checking in, Irene gave the clerk two tickets, one for Alex Pepperberg. Seeing the bird carrier, the agent mentioned that *United Airlines* didn't sell tickets to pets. Despite her arguing, Irene couldn't convince the agent so she asked for her supervisor, who disagreed with the clerk. Seeing three boxes at the bird owner's feet, the agent inquired what they were. Irene replied that this was the luggage for the Grey. When the clerk sarcastically asked, *And I suppose you ordered him a meal?* Irene answered that she had, saying, *He's getting the fruit plate.*

In Tucson, Alex had two other Greys to keep him company, Alo and Kyo. When either of the pair was asked a question, Alex might offer the answer before either of them did, or say, *You're wrong.* In general, Grey Parrots can talk and sound just like their owners. Deborah and Michael Smith have a Grey named Charlie Parker. Deborah related an incident with an obnoxious insurance agent where she wasn't making much progress and was quite frustrated. Charlie knew what was happening so imitating Michael, he said, *I'm going to kick your* ▮▮, *you* ▮▮ ▮ ▮ ▮▮. As you can see, parrots are proficient with different languages.

One experiment that was tried involved linguistic analysis, using sonograms. A technician would be able to identify the speaker as a person. By comparing a human's patterns with that of a parrot, there should be a difference, but the sonograms were very similar. This applied to Alex, a bird that had abilities that he wasn't supposed to have. I said it before, but I'll say it again: this was one smart bird.

Bernd Heinrich worked with ravens and crows. He tied a string almost three feet long to a piece of meat and tied the free end to a tree branch. He wondered if ravens had the intelligence to get the meat. The birds landed on the branch and little by little brought the string up until they had the food. When a similar trial was done with Greys, they did exactly what their cousins had done.

Alex was friendly with some parrots, but not all. The toys that could talk back or played songs really annoyed him. When he encountered one of the former, he was ready to shred it. The talking back doll was removed. Someone sent him a musical toy and he tried to talk to it. Nothing happened. He bent his head over expecting a tickle, just like the lab people would give. Again there was no response. Alex replied, *You turkey*. Apparently, he didn't respect all things whether they could fly or not.

At the end of a typical day, Irene was alone with the birds. Kyo went to his cage, but the trainer ate with Alex and Griffin, another parrot. She had to share and the parrots loved green beans and broccoli. If Griffin had one more bean than Alex, the latter would squawk, with Alex saying, *Green bean*. A similar response came from Griffin if he were shortchanged. After a few days, Alex would utter, *Green*, and Griffin chimed in, *Bean*. They repeated this display with even more gusto.

Alex was terrified of storms, which were quite common in Indiana, especially tornadoes. He was at Pepperberg's home one day when he became upset, saying, *Wanna go back*. There wasn't any storm. Alex had seen two screech owls and was spooked. Irene closed the curtains but that didn't help. She had to take Alex back to the lab. This was the last time he was at the house. That was the only way to calm him down.

Irene was tenured at Arizona University, but even then had no job there when funding was cut for her program. She took sabbaticals and gave presentations back east, some for as long as a year. She could have stayed in Tucson, except she had to teach a biology class, not her specialty. While at a meeting one day, Pepperberg left frustrated because the university left her out in the cold. She came back to the lab, infuriated. Alex could hear her steps and probably saw that she wasn't happy. He didn't whisper, as usual. Instead he said, *Calm down*.

Irene was doing great things, but funding was always a problem. Michael Bove invited her to MIT's Media Lab, which was a nerd's paradise. She spent a year there and continued her work. Alex and some of the other parrots joined her. Because Greys were easily bored, Alex gave wrong answers at times. The project at Media Lab wanted to see if the Internet could keep the birds busy. Fortunately, Alex didn't shred the mouse. The parrots were curious and being online made a difference, even to Alex. They were a few options but our friend opted for the music, grooving to the tunes.

One day Irene received an email with sadness in the subject line. It said that one of the Greys died in the cage. It sounded like Alex the amazing had been the one, and indeed it was. Those in the lab were sad and distressed, especially Pepperberg. It took her days to regain her life. Alex was a star of television, newspapers and magazines. His trainer would be bombarded with sympathy on the phone, in the mail and through emails. So many people knew of the African Grey. There were numerous videos and programs about the smart and smart Alex. Irene felt she had to add more by writing *Alex & Me: How A Scientist And A Parrot Discovered A Hidden World Of Animal Intelligence – And Formed A Deep Bond In The Process*. I highly recommend this book for its laughs and insight.

There are over 300 species of parrots, which are native to Australia, Africa, Central America, Asia and South America. The United States had its own, the Carolina parakeet, but it became extinct in 1918. Parrots come in an assortment of radiant colors: blue, green, red, yellow, purple, black, orange and gray. Most are green. They can be from a few inches to three feet in length, with much of that being the tail. The word *parakeet* describes many different species of parrots with the difference being the length of the tail. Other parrots include cockatiels, lovebirds, Amazons, macaws, rosellas, cockatoos and lories. Other terms for these birds are budgies and conures.

Poaching threatens parrots because of their demand as pets. The young are captured and shipped away to countries demanding them but are packed haphazardly. Great numbers perish on the trip, as many as 60% on route to pet stores. Some new owners grow disappointed with their parakeet since he doesn't talk as much as they had hoped, or his jokes aren't that funny. The result may be to release the bird to make it on his own in a park or rural area. This may have been the case in San Francisco.

Mark Bittner moved from Seattle to Telegraph Hill in that great city. He had no steady job so he struggled for food and a place to sleep, settling on places in the park, on the street or in abandoned buildings. He even slept in a broken down VW van. For food, he might see a dime or quarter on the street and this would be enough to buy a roll. He went to a bakery, put his money on the counter and asked for a roll. The clerk placed one in a bag but then added a few more things. Mark grabbed the bag and left before the sales person said a mistake was made. When he returned a few days later, a different person did the same thing as the first clerk and others repeated the kind gesture. Only one didn't.

One spring, Mark was given the chance to live in a studio apartment in exchange for running errands and housecleaning for a woman named Maxine. He jumped at the chance and worked for her for four years. When Maxine's health failed, her cousin Edna took over her finances and soon placed Maxine in a nearby nursing home. While Edna was selling the home, Mark could move into it and maintain it, staying until it was sold. By this time he became acquainted with dozens of parrots that flew near the house. They were timid at first but Mark soon won them over, even feeding them. A few times the parrots squawked for his attention and food. His knowledge about them grew and he even named them, based on their looks or something they reminded him of. There was Catherine, Connor, Sonny – a bully named after a character in *The Godfather* – Eric, Erica, Lucia, Marlon and Mozart, whose name was soon changed to Costanze, Wolfgang's wife. Bittner gave some of the females names belonging to males and vice versa. In those instances, he came up with an appropriate name. Maybe he should have chosen appellations that were void of gender bias.

When Mandela was flying low, a cat made contact, resulting in the former screaming. Still, he battled and let the feline know that he wouldn't get away with it, but Mandela suffered nerve damage. Bittner put him in a cage and tended to his needs. Mark brought him outside daily, but still the bird bit him, eventually realizing that Bittner was helping him so he backed off. It would take some time for Mandela to heal, but Mark took precautions to make sure his feathered friend would survive when he released him. The day came and Mandela was let go, but after a while Bittner didn't see him. One rainy day, Chomsky flew in for a feeding. Because of the rain, identification of the parrots was a challenge but Mark looked him over. Shortly after that, he saw that the parrot was Mandela and had survived.

One day after feeding, most of the flock left, flying north toward Fisherman's Wharf. Paco hung around for a bit but then decided to join the others. However, he flew east. Soon the mass of parrots changed directions moving southeast. In a short time Paco and the others were together. These creatures are quite intelligent. My account of Irene and Alex earlier should have convinced you that parrots were some of the smartest creatures on the planet. I'm sure Mark's feeling about them mirrored that idea.

The former homeless individual brought other parrots into the house, but only if they needed help. Eventually he hoped to let them go and join the flock. Tupelo, named after the song by Van Morrison, was a juvenile parrot that had been assaulted by other birds and Mark brought her inside, tending to her. The two became close and Morrison's parrot was improving, but one morning she had moved too close to the heater and perished. Bittner was deeply afflicted, realizing how attached he had become with Tupelo. He had witnessed other deaths of the birds, but this instance left him in shambles.

He recovered and felt that he had come a long way since spotting the first parrot. His knowledge was greatly enhanced by talking to veterinarians, scientists and birders. He became involved with photography and even found that computers could be friends, sort of. He became acquainted with Telegraph Hill's history and Bohemian America. He also reduced the time and days he fed the parrots. At the same time he was also writing about Telegraph Hill. Judy Irving contacted him wanting to film the parrots. She was in a relationship but it was going sour. Mark and Judy spent a great deal of time together working on the project. With time they fell in love.

Bittner had done the same thing with Telegraph Hill, San Francisco and the parrots. One day he read Judy a statement of Gary Snyder, after she realized that he had found his place in the country.

The city is just as natural as the country; let's not forget it. There's nothing in the universe that's not natural by definition. One of the poems I like best in 'Turtle Island' is "Night Herons," which is about the naturalness of San Francisco.

Bittner had to find a new place to live and found one in the home of friends in Piedmont, who said he could stay for as long as it took to finish his book. After a year, he moved to a real house, part of a compound of cabins. Judy moved in with him but the compound was soon on the market. The pair figured that the solution was to buy the compound but developers outbid them. Eventually, their deal fell through and after fifteen months and three attempts, Judy and Mark got the property.

Mark wrote the book, *The Wild Parrots Of Telegraph Hill: A Love Story – With Wings*. Thanks to Judy, a documentary of the same name came around the same time.

I mentioned Sy and Howard earlier and their farm in New England. They live there with all kinds of animals, and love those creatures. Sy is like a veterinarian without the practice, as well as a vegetarian. There may have been some animal at the dinner table in her kitchen, but never on a platter covered with gravy. Montgomery encountered many different species on her numerous nature trips abroad. In and around her home lived a flock of chickens. Sy and Howard purchased chicks but only two roosters, so far. On occasion the newly bought batch of chicks included some of the males. They all got along although the roosters could be bossy at times. Chickens are smart creatures although they do some strange things at times. This applies even to those that are not factory farm fowl.

One of Sy's brood was Pickles, who was somewhat challenged. After she suffered an injury she was given a collar similar what cats wear after being neutered. To keep away from the others, Pickles was relegated to the bathroom downstairs, where she stayed on the sink's edge. This setup in the bathroom resulted in not many guests being very happy about this bird watching them.

For a while Bobbie and Jarvis were tenants on the farm. They had their own chickens, who hung out near the kitchen window. Bobbie discovered why. The birds heard the classical music on the radio in the kitchen and stayed close to the sound. With the music turned off, the chicks moved near the picnic table. I wonder if they would have hung around for the notes of Charlie Parker. Another tenant was Elizabeth Kenney who loved animals and also had her own flock. Some of the birds spoke in a voice that was only for Liz. This resulted in her being given the name of *the Chicken Whisperer*. She called, *C'mon, Janny, c'mon boit-boit*. Jan then sat on Elizabeth's legs while the owner quietly whisped: *Boit-boit-boit*. The hen softly responded, *Boit-boit-boit*.

Some chickens hatch and immediately know how to walk, scratch, run and peck. They also follow the first moving object in their vision. You could just turn out to be a *mother*. Studies have shown that an average chicken can recognize more than a hundred others of its kind. Yeah, but can they remember their names? In one experiment, chickens were given a reward if they pecked at a certain button. They received more if they waited with their pecking, which they did. This behavior happened 90 percent of the time. One thing that is not missing from chickens is smarts.

At six foot and 150 pounds, you won't find a bigger bird than the cassowary. Found in North Queensland, Australia, it won't win any beauty contest despite its brilliant color. No other bird murders more humans, thanks to its three pronged feet. Each has a dagger-like claw that can kill. Despite this, Sy was on a trip hoping to spot one. That wasn't an easy task since the cassowary is so elusive. You can be in an area with the monster a few feet away and not even know it's there.

Not unexpectedly, Sy saw plenty of wildlife but no cassowaries. It was the last day of her trip, so she gave it another try. She hiked up Bicton Hill and once again failed to see a cassowary. There may have been one nearby, but those beasts are sly. Around noon she tried once more but had to be on a bus that left at 3:30 in the afternoon heading to the airport. Again there was no cassowary sighting so Sy had to admit that her search was over. Maybe someone was smiling down on her since the bus departure was delayed until 5 pm because of skydivers who weren't through with their exercises. This gave her a few more minutes. This time she came almost face to face with Clyde the cassowary. Her trip was a success.

Hummingbirds are infinitesimally smaller than Clyde. From the family *Trochilidae*, they are among the smallest birds, usually about three to five inches in size. The smallest is a species from Cuba, the bee hummingbird, which is almost weightless. Sy helped her friend, Brenda Sherburn take care of a pair of chicks on the west coast. At birth they were about the size of a kidney bean. One was two days older than the other, and that's how they identified them. Names weren't meant to be given to hummingbirds since people thought that doing so would result in caretakers becoming too close to the birds.

Brenda was saddled with the task of feeding the two young birds every twenty minutes. The meals consist of fresh or frozen fruit flies, which her husband, Russ, handled. The only break came when the hummingbirds were sleeping. If a feeding cycle is missed, the birds can expire. Too much food and they can explode. After a few days, the birds were doing so well that Brenda and Sy agreed to name them after all. The older became Maya and the younger Zuni. Once the two were older, they'd have to catch their own fruit flies and gather nectar from blossoms.

Full-grown hummingbirds can fly backwards, upside down and they can hover. They also have to eat often since they beat their wings at 60 times per second, which requires great amounts of energy. Diving out of the sky, some of these birds can move at over 60 miles an hour. Based on their size, the Allen's hummingbird is the fastest bird in the world, diving at 385 body lengths per second compared to 200 for a peregrine falcon and 207 for the space shuttle.

A mother hummingbird must depart the nest for food for her young ten to 100 times a day. She has to get tired. A hummingbird needs fifteen hundred flower visits and about 600 insects daily. If a human were as active as a hummingbird, he would require 155,000 calories a day. Consuming those calories would result in the human's body temperature reaching 700 degrees Fahrenheit. I mentioned the shuttle earlier and ignition comes to mind, just like what would happen to the man. It may be a good idea to stay away from the buffet.

Because of the energy demands, a hummingbird must eat every fifteen minutes or so. They have to store up enough fat to be able to fly 500 miles across the Gulf of Mexico. If these birds still don't impress you, consider their trips south. They need food so they fly to Central America and South America in winter. Those who reside in the tropics or friendly confines of the American south may not move south of the equator. Some species travel to southern Alaska or the Yukon in spring. Anyway you see it, that is some journey and they do it without GPS.

Montgomery wrote about her experiences with all the mentioned creatures in her book, *Birdology: Adventures With A Pack Of Hens, A Peck Of Pigeons, Cantankerous Crows, Fierce*

Falcons, Hip Hop Parrots, Baby Hummingbirds, And One Murderously Big Living Dinosaur.

Stacey O'Brien inherited her love of animals from her father, who worked at the Jet Propulsion Laboratories. She went to school at Occidental College, attending classes at Caltech and received a degree in biology from the former school in 1985. She and her sister, Gloria, were actors as children and also sang on numerous record albums, in commercials and movies. Most likely you heard them but didn't realize it was the duo.

Before graduating, Stacey had a part-time job at Caltech's Institute of Behavior Biology concerning primates. This was followed by a full time job, studying owls. One day a young owlet needed a home and she was offered the chance to be a foster parent. The little guy was only a few days old and she accepted the mission. She could study owl behavior for some time since the owl couldn't be released into the wild since he had an injured wing. She brought the critter home on Valentines Day and called him Wesley.

She discovered that owls lived to the age of about fifteen or twenty years in captivity. Then she heard about feeding. Owls survive on one and only one source of food: mice. The father hunts for them and has quite a job since each child needs six rodents per day. Don't forget that he also needs some for himself and his mate. If there are five babies, he has to catch over three-dozen mice, no easy task.

Wesley's hunter would be Stacey but fortunately, she could buy them, dead or alive. She killed some and discovered a way to end their lives so the victim wouldn't suffer. Rats were another option. Because of their size, they had to be cut up. This could be done on frozen rats as they could be sliced into owl-sized morsels. If an owl is fed any other diet, he won't survive. Wesley would need all the nutrients supplied by the mice, which he swallowed whole. His saliva did the trick of digesting his prey, and quickly – say in an hour. Certain parts such as the bones and fir became part of a pellet that owls expelled.

Humans rely on visual means for observation; dogs have a remarkable sense of smell; owls had a keen sense of hearing. They don't use echolocation like bats or dolphins, but hone in through a *sound picture* of all the other animals and nature's sounds. This is done though the conjunction of the satellite-dish face of the owl, brain involvement and ear placement: one ear is high up and the other lower. A mouse beneath three feet of snow can't hide from an owl if the former has a heartbeat.

Besides the unusual placement of ears, owls can do some strange things. They can manipulate their skin and create different looks, which has to be kind of spooky. With their long necks, they have the ability to rotate their head a bit more than 180°. As you guess, this can freak people out. One time Wesley faced Stacey over his back. When she realized the situation, she admonished him, *Wesley, don't scare me like that!* He must have seen *The Exorcist* too many times.

O'Brien managed the task of mouse management for Wesley, but she had plenty of adventures. Even though she wasn't thrilled about the butcher business, she picked some live mice and put them in the back seat of her car in a paper bag. She needed gas so she pulled into a station and was about to talk to the attendant, when she noticed the expression on his face after he gazed into the car. She knew what was happening. The mice were running around and she had to capture them. She didn't round them all up and some wrecked havoc on her car. One died in the car and Stacey had to put up with the stench for a while, driving with the windows open.

Stacey lived with her friend Wendy, renting a room. The house was soon to have stately visitors so they cleaned, prepared for their guests and cleaned some more. Naturally, the owl lady had concerns because of Wesley and his food. Again she had some live ones and she put them in the bathroom. She went to help Wendy for a while and returned to notice that two had escaped. The guests arrived and Stacey found one of the escapees in the drier, whom she rescued and released. The other was still AWOL. On the second day, Stacey found some black poop outside the guest room. Before long the lady visiting opened the door and inquired of her, *Excuse me, have you lost a mouse?* Stacey replied that she had but then realized that he was in the guest's room. This visitor wasn't bothered at all and said, *You know, many people keep owls in England.* There was a great deal of concern for naught.

Owls are so dedicated that they mate for life. If one of the pair dies, the other is deeply affected by it. He or she may get depressed and soon die as well. Stacey had her feathered friend but dated a few guys – or at least met them. The names aren't important. One wasn't crazy about nature so that didn't last. Another was jealous of the bird, so that one didn't work out, either. If it wasn't Wesley, it had to do with what nourished him: the mice. In a way, her owl guided her to choose someone who he approved of.

Stacey went to the hospital and had emergency surgery. In her absence, Wendy looked after Wesley, who accepted his temporary caretaker. This can be attributed to how smart Wesley was, realizing that Stacey was ailing. He may even have known she was in the hospital. When she returned, she was homebound for two months of recuperation. She didn't mind as she would be with the owl and could use the rest. Wesley was happy, too.

Stacey never trained Wesley to talk, but spoke to him just like a parent did to a child. After a while, her pet knew what she was saying and responded accordingly. If she offered him a *mice* – she didn't use the singular because owls are bad with grammar – he understood. If Wesley was starving, he showed it by his response. When he was full, he would turn his head and she knew he had enough to eat. If she said they would play in two hours, he sensed when it was *playtime*. If she forgot, he reminded her. They communicated and did it well even though he didn't speak. He made plenty of noises, some quite alarming.

Stacey would later learn that her grandmother also had a barn owl. Weisel, whose name was really similar to Wesley, also couldn't survive in the wild so both grandparents were caretakers. Her grandma died and Stacey found out about Weisel from her grandpa, who was some kind of cousin to Stacey's pet, obviously.

This isn't the end of the story. For more insight about owls, Wesley and Stacey, read her book, *Wesley The Owl: The Remarkable Love Story Of An Owl And His Girl*. It's very entertaining. I will relate one other incident about Wesley. As he aged, his talons needed to be trimmed – they were bothering his master. His beak grew as well and was a concern, needing filing. Of course, Stacey's animal friend wasn't thrilled about what this involved. She talked to him, mentioning what she would do and assured him that it was necessary. She would not hurt him. Stacey conversed this way for a few days. When the day of the trimming occurred, Wesley accepted the process, trusting in Stacey. The talons and beak were filed down. The two of them had a very special relationship.

I'll talk more about an incredible eagle later, but for now mention that the bald version is the national symbol of our country. There aren't too many people who have anything against the eagle. The pigeon isn't so lucky as many are in awe of them but more people despise them. Pigeons of any kind may be the Rodney Dangerfield of all birds – they get no respect. The haters might change their mind if they knew more about them. Of course they leave deposits on buildings and people – most likely on those who don't like them. The Egyptians used those droppings as an effective nitrogen-rich manure. Other nations utilized it as well and in some cases guards were set up to keep thieves away from it. In England, the poop was declared property of the crown. Pigeons are not a health hazard and also not filthy. We shouldn't forget that they go back centuries and have contributed to society in many ways, which I'll mention later.

Many of the anti-pigeonites take part in poisoning them – not exactly the way Tom Lehrer mentioned in a song from the 1950s, "Poisoning Pigeons in the Park". They're exterminators, using the real stuff as part of a lucrative business. Others participate in pigeon shoots. Sure, you have the hunters who'll bag one of the birds every so often. Maybe they need something for dinner. The shoots I mean are organized and illegal in most states. That doesn't stop their occurrence. These events are more difficult to find.

Shooting or poisoning may eliminate a few pigeons but each is the wrong approach. The extermination idea is really dumb as it can kill the predators of the creatures they just murdered. Doing that could mean even more pigeons, rather than fewer. Do you still think that method makes sense? Poison in the air has never been a good idea. The other idea isn't any better, as witnessed by a writer who infiltrated one of the shoots. Andrew Blechman was working on a book about pigeons and thought he might do some shooting. After some great effort, he found a place, saw how it went and fired some shots. His observations accomplished two things: shoots don't work but can turn a pacifist into one who doesn't mind joining the fray.

Blechman missed time and again but finally hit the target, just grazing it. As he was more successful with each firing, he felt an adrenalin rush, wanting to prove something to those watching. Luckily, he stopped but observed that this approach was really brutal. During pigeon shoots, some escaped without being hit. The others weren't so lucky. A few were wounded but soon perished. Others fled to the forest and then died. All suffered greatly. Even if the method had some merit there was too much madness and was illegal, or should be everywhere.

I've already alluded to pigeon control by not using extermination. Predators might do their part. Another idea which could be used – maybe it was tried – was some kind of birth control. Forget the two ideas of killing and look instead at some progressive ideas.

David Roth lives in Phoenix and cares for the belittled birds. To use the word squalor for the place he lives in is being way too kind. Use your imagination. Nevertheless, he's involved because he sees their suffering. The Maricopa County jail isn't kind to the residents – the sheriff in 1993 thought baloney sandwiches were fine for lunch and pink underwear was acceptable too. Perhaps his brother was in the business. The Arizona jail had pigeons in the thousands, but outside. Brilliant minds thought the poison idea was the answer. Roth suggested netting, which would keep the creatures away. It would be an idea that would work and save money – a great deal. David's idea was so successful that a decade later the netting appeared to be brand-new and no pigeons lingered.

The netting led the pigeons elsewhere, and there were huge numbers. In the early nineteenth century, John James Audubon reported seeing a great many flying overhead in a patch that seemed endless, enough to have an eclipse type effect. It was some swarm. Besides the mentioned methods of control, there was a suggestion of a catch-and-release program. If you don't know about pigeon racing, it's a sport where a few of them are driven miles away, 200 or 300 or more, to an unfamiliar place and they have to get home. And they do, somehow using magnetic fields in the process. I doubt that the catch-and-release would work.

Why not outlaw pigeon feeding, both scraps and birdseed? It would help except for the commuter who dropped his bagel remnant before hopping on the train. That's littering, so just like the feeder, he could be fined. Both could then be made to sit in a lawn chair under the swarm. As far as placating participants in the shoots, what about using clay pigeons or lawyers? Don't email or write me, Shakespeare had the idea first. I'm just adopting it to the twenty-first century. We really need innovative ideas, and they work.

Pigeons have been domesticated since the dawn of man. In 776 B.C., one of the birds carried news of the Olympics; centuries later one heralded the news from Waterloo about Napoleon. Millions of the despised birds served in World War I and World War II, gathering intelligence and saving many lives. They were also used in the Gulf War. Darwin's research for the theory of evolution utilized pigeons.

They can fly 500 miles in a day and reach speeds of over 60 miles per hour. They have been known to remain aloft for as long as sixteen hours. They have an outstanding sense of hearing, able to detect infrasound as low as a single hertz. Humans can't hear anything below twenty hertz. These birds can recognize 26 letters of the alphabet.

Press Clay Southworth, a teenager in Ohio, spotted a beautiful bird that he didn't recognize at the turn of the twentieth century. He couldn't take a picture so instead he shot the last passenger pigeon in the wild. A local taxidermist stuffed the dead animal, using buttons for eyes and hence the name given him. On the first day of September fourteen years later, the last passenger pigeon in captivity died in the Cincinnati Zoo. Martha was 29.

What's this fuss I hear about an Eagle Rights Amendment? Why I think the eagle has been treated fair enough. . . . Between you and me, if we give eagles rights, the next thing you know, we'll have to give rights to pigeons. . . . Why, you won't be able to get a seat in the park. It will be the birds sitting on the benches throwing us little pieces of toast. – Emily Litella on *Weekend Update*

Blechman's book, *Pigeons: The Fascinating Saga Of The World's Most Revered And Reviled Bird*, sets the record straight on these much-maligned birds. I mentioned the Seals and Crofts song, "Hummingbird" earlier. Maybe I should have titled the chapter, "The House at Pooh Corner". That covers everything.

7. Teddy Bears Picnic

One of the songs I heard growing up was the old song given by the chapter title. It was written by John Walter Bratton in 1907. It was only in 1932 that a vocal version of the song appeared. Performed by a few artists including Bing Crosby and Jerry Garcia, I have a rousing version done by the Nitty Gritty Dirt Band on cassette. As you might guess, this chapter deals primarily with bears.

By now it should be obvious that four-legged animals – for the most part – get along quite well with two-legged ones. This may not be exactly true during hunting season, but even then, those carrying rifles admire wild turkeys and deer, and many enjoy just being out in the woods away from civilization. Those men and women probably find being up in a tree stand to be exhilarating. A family's relationship with Fang or Garfield is a loving one – extending both ways. Each member of the venture obtains something from it. As we have seen, a child offers the family beagle love as well as water and food. In turn, this creature brings calmness and has a soothing effect on the owner and his or her family.

An outstanding Canadian movie about working together – people with other people and humans with the animal kingdom – is the 2005 movie, *Spirit Bear: The Simon Jackson Story*. Karmode bears, known as *spirit bears*, are cream-colored and not albino bears nor of the family of polar bears. They are related to the North American black bear of British Columbia. At times a black mother can produce a white cub because of recessive genes.

Based on real-life events, this inspirational motion picture is the story of a fifteen-year old boy, who when being preyed upon in the wilds of British Columbia, is saved by a Kermode bear. Soon Simon realizes that this rare white bear is endangered by the lumbering industry, with only 400 of these magnificent animals left in the region. The corporation is out to destroy the very place that Spirit Bear calls home.

It makes a convincing argument that one person can affect change. This young political activist is deeply inspired not only by the white bear, but by others around him. They in turn may have lost hope but instead are motivated by Simon, who stood up to the forest industry. These companies have so many places to harvest wood, and could do so without so much devastation to resources and wildlife if only they acted in an environmentally sound way, instead of clear cutting.

Simon's task is formidable, as he is up against not only the powerful forest industry but also the provincial government. The Backstreet Boys and Prince William joined the movement and the result is 2500 square miles being saved on Princess Royal Island. Not many large land protection battles won have been more significant. For his leadership, Simon was recognized by *Time Magazine* as a *Hero for the Planet.*

Spirit Bear illustrates the connection between man and animal. It also gives us hope and should convince each of us that we can make a difference. Obviously if a group joins in to help, matters will be that much easier to accomplish any goal. People and animals feed on each other – I don't mean it that way. In any event, it won't be easy, but great things can be accomplished. They probably wouldn't have been involved without that first initiation by a single individual.

Ruth Elizabeth McCombs was born in September 1900 in Titusville, Pennsylvania. Despite living in the place where the first oil well was drilled, her family wasn't poor but not rich, either. William Harvest Harkness, Jr. hailed from a wealthy New York family, but not connected to the Standard Oil clan. The family did have an estate in Connecticut, though. The two met in Manhattan while in their early twenties and noticed each other instantly. They were bohemians and weren't bothered by Prohibition, as they quickly discovered the speakeasies. Both were seekers of adventure with Ruth having two things she hated: *going to bed at night* and *waking in the morning.*

Ruth managed one semester at the University of Colorado and then taught English in Cuba before landing in New York. Bill graduated from Harvard in 1924 and embarked on journeys to different corners of the globe. In the spring of 1934, the Harvard graduate and his associates brought back a few Komodo dragons from Indonesia. Though just as close as married, Ruth and Bill didn't wed until September 9, 1934, in a small civil ceremony. Soon Bill headed off on a three-year hunting excursion. Naturally,

Ruth wanted to be there with him. At the time, there were trips by different people to capture animals for zoos and also for stuffing. Frank Buck supposedly delivered 10,000 mammals and 100,000 birds from the wilds. Many of those numbers died on the way to the United States.

On February 19, 1936, outside Shanghai, Bill Harkness was in a hospital, dying of cancer. He and his associate Floyd Tangier Smith were stuck there. Because of his heavy drinking and smoking, Bill died, leaving Ruth a grieving widow. At first she couldn't believe that he had died, but when it was confirmed, it affected her deeply. Eventually she felt that she had to finish what her husband had been doing in his search for the panda. Less than two months after Bill's death, she was headed east to London and Paris on board the liner *American Trader*. She departed Paris with Gerry Russell who went with her to China on board the *Tancred*. It was fortunate that Russell came along insofar as Ruth had no experience of being in these far off places. Her friends thought she was crazy since she never walked in New York if a taxi was on the scene. Floyd Smith, an associate of her husband was in China and could have been of assistance to her.

Arriving in the Far East, despite the decadence, noise, smell and absence of morals, Shanghai impressed her with its huge skyscrapers. This was a place where Communism met capitalism. After spending some time with Smith, she felt he was as useful as the comatose 113th U. S. Congress. Floyd seemed to be along for the ride and for Bill's money when he was *working* with him. In her eyes, Russell wasn't much better. She let them both go when she met a few others. Jack Young and Dan Reib really knew what they were doing, but the former had another commitment. His brother Quentin was younger but had a great deal of promise, so he and Dan were on board with her. Quentin was engaged to Diana Chen but that didn't keep the sparks from flying between him and Ruth.

They would begin hunting in a region southwest of Chengdu. At the time, China was overcome with political struggles, with the communists fighting the Kuomintang. It was a difficult time for foreigners as well as locals. The panda pursuit was fraught with concerns since these 400-pound animals survived almost exclusively on bamboo. These bears had survived for millions of years. The expedition of Ruth and her crew began in late September 1936 when they boarded the steamer *Whangpu*, heading up the Long River. They then boarded the *Mei Ling*, which would bring them to Chungking. Once they departed the Yangtze, they had to be concerned about bandits, wild animals, the heat and the environment, where they had to climb up steep slopes and go through dense bamboo filled brush. The excursion was planned to cover over two-dozen miles per day.

She may have been on the adventure of her life, but Ruth wanted no part of killing any panda, since she loved all animals. For a short stretch, the party had some protection and she even had some practice shooting, although she and guns never got along. She was asked to carry a gun but usually refused to do so. From what she had managed in target practice, she was led to believe *That she should not be trusted with a weapon of any kind.*

Besides Young and Reib, the group had sixteen coolies and a cook, Wang Whai Hsin. There'd be a few more who joined the venture, even if only for part of the journey. She may not have had the outdoor experience, but she had people who could help her achieve her goal. Though she paid for Russell's return home, he was actually on the trail ahead of her in the pursuit of the panda, reporting to his partner in Shanghai, the hospitalized Smith.

Because of her determination and the resourcefulness of the crew, they brought a baby giant panda into the camp, judged to be about a week old. At birth, a panda only weighs a few ounces. Called Baby at first, this find was later renamed Su-Lin after Jack's wife. Now they had to feed him and bring him to Shanghai – no easy task. Ruth and Quentin gave him nourishment and nurtured him and they arrived in the city in November of the same year they began the excursion. The one bad thing was that Su-Lin was taken away from his mother.

Pandas are also known as giant pandas or panda bears and not related to the red panda, which lives in the Communist part of China. That figures. Pandas have been known to live as long forty years or longer if well cared for, although their average life is twenty-five years in captivity. In the wild, scientists haven't determined their lifespan. The weight of a male can be as much as 350 pounds, but averaging about 230 pounds. The female registers from 170 to 270 pounds.

As Su-Lin grew, the next challenge Ruth and Quentin was to transport the baby panda to a zoo in the United States. Because Ruth had used the idea that it's better to do something and then apologize later rather than seek permission, she was delayed boarding the ship home. She was all set when politics left her behind. Finally she was on her way with the giant panda. Her plan was to give Baby to a zoo that would finance her next journey in the Far East. She had no takers until Su-Lin joined the *Brookfield Zoo* in Chicago. After a while it was discovered that Su-Lin was a male.

Harkness returned to China the next year for another panda, but it wasn't the same with Quentin's absence and China being attacked by the Japanese. Nevertheless, in December she had another baby panda, Mei-Mei, who was three times the size of Su-Lin when he was found. In the years that followed she saw the suffering of the pandas as they were being captured as well as those who had perished along the way. Then she realized she was almost doing the same thing in her pursuits. Her leaving China with Mei-Mei was easier than her previous departure with Baby and soon the two pandas were together at the *Brookfield Zoo*. On Friday April 1, 1938, Su-Lin died of pneumonia.

Ruth eventually returned to Manhattan and did some writing for magazines, even giving up drinking, which she had done too often. Then she went back into partying and her health suffered for it. Around the end of July 1947, she was found dead in her bathtub in her hotel, reportedly of acute alcoholic gastro-enteritis. Haskness had written, *The Lady And The Panda: An Adventure*, *The Baby Giant Panda* and *Pangoan Diary*. Many other books have been written about Ruth and the pandas, including one I thoroughly recommend, *The Lady And The Panda: The True Adventures Of The First American Explorer To Bring Back China's Most Exotic Animal* by Vicky Croke. The author researched letters written by Harkness and ones from her close friend Hazel Perkins. Relatives of Perkins, Reib and the Youngs provided great insight into the incredible lady explorer.

You may have heard of another bear explorer, Dr. Ian Stirling, who earned biology degrees from the University of British Columbia in Vancouver as well as a Ph.D. from New Zealand's Canterbury University. His research on the polar bear in the Arctic encompassed about 40 years as he explained their evolution and behavior. Stirling has written three books on the animal including, *Polar Bears: A Natural History Of A Threatened Species.*

When children see a koala bear, they want to have one as a pet, replacing their stuffed teddy bear, whose ear was chewed off. They're young so they don't realize that there aren't any eucalyptus trees in the back yard, which is what these bears need as nourishment. Found in Australia, they sleep as many as twenty hours a day but are antisocial, becoming dependent on the mother and siblings.

No matter what the type of bear is, polar, spirit, black, brown, panda or koala – but not teddy – many people can't get close enough to the creature. In Yellowstone Park, a father may want a family member to get up-close so he can take a photo for Facebook. It's not that great an idea, rather a terrible one. All bears are wild animals, possessing sharp claws and they can hurt humans. Bringing one home as a pet can never be recommended. Adventurers and scientists who come upon a cub that is either abandoned by his or her mother – maybe the latter was killed by a poacher – may be better off doing nothing to save the abandoned baby as other bears may take care of him or her. In the event that the cub is rescued and rehabilitated, the best that can happen is for the animal to be restored to the wild.

In the summer of 2014, I saw part of a nature program on polar bears in Canada, which showed an overpopulation of bears. This seemed to refute the idea of global warming. Maybe I didn't see enough of that feature since ice in the Arctic has been melting faster in the last decade than usual. Sea levels have been rising and islands have been disappearing simultaneously. Record high temperatures have been posted over the last ten years and then have been broken again – all over the world. Do you think that hurricanes Katrina and Sandy were the result of global warming? Moreover, Dr. Stirling, who I mentioned earlier, conducted studies of polar bears in Western Hudson Bay and confirmed the existence of global warming, with the population of these bears dropping 22% since 1987.

Maybe these people denying this weather change are smoking something – I don't want any of it. More likely, they're not scientists or of the junk variety. It's time to be reasonable.

Either it's happening or it isn't. It has to be one or the other. Let's suppose it really is happening and we take serious action to rectify global warming. We might make a difference. On the other hand, if nothing is done, life will be very difficult as the days march on. If global warming is not occurring, doing something won't hurt in the least and may even be beneficial. If we take the lazy approach, we might still be all right, but the inattention could lead to future global warming. I think precaution and working now is the recommended approach. You can read more about it in the book by Naomi Oreskes and Erik M. Conway, *Merchants Of Doubt: How A Handful Of Scientists Obscured The Truth On Issues From Tobacco Smoke To Global Warming*. I doubt that the junkies have read the book.

8. Old Blue

Chris walks into a pet shop, looking to buy a dog. Sean, the owner, tells his about his wonder dog, Fang.

What's so special about him? Chris asks.

Sean replied, *He's smarter than some people, especially lawyers, salesmen or politicians. I'll ask him a question. What covers a house?*

Roof, came the reply from Fang.

Chris smiled but wasn't convinced, so Sean continues with the question, *How does sandpaper feel?*

Ruff.

To that answer, Chris begins to leave.

Hating to lose a sale, Sean asks Chris to wait a minute as he had one last question for Fang. *Who was the greatest baseball player that ever lived?*

When Fang responded, *Ruth,* Chris departed.

Fang then looked at Sean and says, *Maybe I should have said Josh Gibson, but I have problems with two-syllable words.*

That may be a joke, but the intelligence of canines certainly isn't.

When you're away
I sit her and mope.
Won't you come home,
You big dope?

Don't blame me for the poem above – I'm not a poet. The four lines showed up a few years ago in a Valentine card for Pat, who shared a modified a-frame with Barron, his loyal German shepherd, Harry and me. The three us were teachers in downstate New York. I didn't write those four lines. Maybe Barron enlisted in a writing class or Harry tutored him in English. Harry claimed he didn't pen the poem. I doubt that Barron did the writing and I didn't either. This was one of a few adventures with this canine.

At the time, teachers weren't that well paid so the three of us did a great deal of cooking. I recall the time we worked together making marinated eggplant. It involved a great amount of effort, even though there were only a few ingredients: eggplant, olive oil, garlic, vinegar and salt. The result was delicious and the culinary delights were also evident one day when we had a roast of beef. We didn't eat it all, but made a big mistake when we left the house that day. It remained on the counter and Barron wasn't a vegetarian. You get the picture.

Some time after that, I decided to make some cannoli. Somehow I obtained the aluminum tubes – these had nothing to do with weapons of mass destruction (WMD) – so I started making the shells. It was a good start and the filling was next. I chose to add some chocolate bits, which had to be mixed in to the other ingredients. Using the blender to do that wasn't a good idea as the result was watery, making filling the shells difficult. For the three amigos to throw food away was a rare occurrence, so we did some dipping. Barron didn't partake of the dessert, but he did carry an unfilled shell up to the loft, where Pat slept. He laid it gently on Pat's bed, just for his master.

Barron was not like some watchdogs that sit around and *watch* as burglars vandalize a house. When Harry and I first met this German shepherd, Pat had done a superb job of training him and we all got along very well. Anyone approaching our temporary residence when we were away would have departed quickly after a few menacing barks. Friends of ours who visited us were treated much better and didn't have to worry about getting tetanus shots afterwards.

Leland Duncan was born in 1893 in California to Elizabeth and Grant Duncan. Three years after that his sister Marjorie came into the world. Before the century ended, Grant left and wasn't heard from again. Lee's father may have died from a burst appendix. Soon the children were left at the *Fred Finch Children's Home* since Elizabeth couldn't raise her son and daughter on her own. The century ended in a depression as well.

Lee had been abandoned and survived despite what happened. He and his sister were only in the children's home for three years. Lee was affected by *Finch* in a good way and would never forget where he had been for that time. The Duncans moved

88

in with Elizabeth's parents. The boy's grandfather had ranch dogs, but Lee was kept away from them. His first dog, Jack, a small terrier, came later and Lee was thrilled. He discovered he liked dogs and could work with them. An Airedale named Firefly was another of his dogs and Lee was involved in breeding her, selling the little ones.

When Duncan was seventeen, he entered the army. After some training in Texas, Lee departed the boat in Glasgow for a train to England. In the war, about sixteen million animals were used: camels, horses, mules, oxen, pigeons and dogs. About a third of the animals were dogs, many donated by the citizenry. Canines were used for many missions and a few had a label placed on their necks that said, *useless*. Most of these were shot. Max Emil Friedrich von Stephanitz was responsible for breeding German shepherds near the end of the nineteenth century. It soon became a familiar dog.

Lee found himself in France in Fluiry when he entered a building that served as a kennel. To his shock, he saw over twenty massacred dogs. He also found two pigeons, which he released. He heard whimpering dogs and discovered a female German shepherd with five puppies, which he brought to safety. He gave the mother and three of the puppies to fellow soldiers, keeping a female and male for himself. Bringing the two puppies home was a challenge but eventually he arrived in New York with them. His next task was to take them to California by train. Nanette had to stay behind because of sickness, but Mrs. Leo Wanner would take care of her until she recovered, at which time she could join Lee and the male puppy, who had another puppy as a companion. Sadly Nanette died.

The male puppy grew and was strong even though he was undersized. In a competition with a shepherd named Marie, Rinty cleared the wall, which was almost twelve feet high, while his opponent's back paws struck the top. Acquaintance Charley Jones filmed the event and Lee received a $350 check for it from *Novagraph*, a newsreel company. Lee chose the name of Rin Tin Tin for his dog, based on one half of a pair of survivors from a Paris railway bombing. The survivor's companion's name was Nanette, which Lee also gave to the puppy that accompanied his puppy to the west coast. Other names for Lee's shepherd were Rin-

Tin-Tin, Rin-tin-tin, Rinty and Rin. The canine soon was on his way to Hollywood, thanks to Jones. Lee wrote screenplays, including *Where the North Begins*. Rinty managed quite well in silent films – the talkies were a few years away.

Rinty's first role was in the *Man from Hell's River*, followed by a small part in *My Dad*. The dog landed the leading role in *Where the North Begins,* which Warner Brothers produced. Rinty wasn't the first dog star, but he was inspired by Strongheart and soon many others followed including Fang, Ace the Wonder Dog, Wolfheart and Flash. Film critic Carl Sandberg said that Rinty was *Phenomenal* and *thrillingly intelligent*. A fan wrote, *Rin Tin Tin registers more range of emotion than any other dog actor known to the screen has attained*. His films brought in so much money that he was paid more than seven times what the human actors received. Rinty even had his own radio show, *The Wonder Dog*. He was a character in books such as *The Little Folks' Story Of Rin Tin Tin*.

Just as actors have stunt doubles, many of the German shepherds people saw in Rinty's flicks were look-alikes. This practice occurred for years. Similarly, when the talkies premiered in the late 1920s, many actors didn't make the transition. Rinty also was given his walking papers but he still captured the imagination of adults and children. He had more to do, obtaining fewer dollars but staying on the silver screen in the talkies. Lee took him on the vaudeville circuit and there were numerous tours. Some of these dogs were the original Rinty, but many were his offspring or other German shepherds that just wanted to be part of the family. Lee and Rin Tin Tin – or some German shepherd – performed for children and Lee often mentioned his days at *Fred Finch*, stopping there and doing it on the first stop of the tour.

In the summer of 1932, Old Rin died. Death notices were posted in theaters, newspapers and *Movietone's* newsreel. He was deeply missed but descendants filled the role with the same success. Bert Leonard came along with television and soon Rinty had a new medium, in which he flourished, just like the others. The program, *The Adventures of Rin Tin Tin* premiered on ABC-TV on October 15, 1954 with overwhelming praise. In television history, few shows surpassed it in climbing to the top of the ratings. It was broadcast in 70 other countries and just about everybody knew the dog's name.

There will always be a Rin Tin Tin. Born in France at the time of World War I – which resulted in a million orphans in France – he has never died and will go on forever. Susan Orlean spent years researching the Rin Tin Tin story, which covered almost a century. She talked to descendents, associates and friends of Duncan, but no German shepherd was interviewed. She wrote a book about the dog, *Rin Tin Tin: The Life And The Legend.*

A five-year old untrained German shepherd named Buddy, who is a resident of the city of Anchorage, Alaska, showed how smart he is in the spring of 2010. Ben Heinrichs encountered a fire on his land. His clothes caught fire, but he put it out by rolling in the snow. Knowing of the danger, Buddy summoned help. Alaska State Trooper Terrence Shanigan spotted our hero and followed him to the scene. Ben was slightly injured but without Buddy, the Heinrichs family would have lost their home. The latter knew that this German shepherd was gifted because on other occasions, he scared bears away while Ben was hunting. For his outstanding service, our hero received a big rawhide bone and a stainless steel dog bowl.

Another really smart German shepherd is Rex, also known as Rexy and Sergeant Rex. As you guessed it, he was in the armed services, even attending boot camp. He stayed with a family as a puppy, but only for a short time before he left for training. Eventually he met Sergeant Mike Dowling at Camp Pendleton in Southern California, but only growled at Mike. Dowling soon won Rex over and they became part of a K9 team. These duos were used in Vietnam and would be deployed to Iraq in the early twenty-first century. Besides German shepherds, Belgian Malinoise, or *Mals*, and Dutch shepherds are used by the Marine Corps for K9 teams.

Mike hailed from Richmond, California, and loved animals when he was young, with pets Murphy the Irish setter and the cocker spaniel, Brandy. Dowling worked with a Labrador named August at *Guiding Eyes for the Blind*. He thought about joining the Marines but went to the University of California at Santa Barbara, soon flunking out. Joining the Marines he was soon to meet Rex. As mentioned earlier, dogs have an amazing sense of smell and can detect explosives and munitions, saving lives. Rex and Mike were sent to Iraq in 2004 to find Improvised Explosive Devices (IEDs). They stayed throughout the country, starting out in Mahmoudiyah, the Triangle of Death, but also spending time in Fallujah.

Rex was a small shepherd, but he was handsome. People commented on that and the children loved him. Just like Rex had needed time to accept Mike, anyone else who came close to him would hear growling and may even have been bitten. That happened often. The dog needed assurance from Dowling to be calmed during explosions and gunfire. He could detect the nasty stuff, though. A mechanical bomb-detection device could detect too, but not as good as a dog. The canine was much more efficient since you could talk to him. He could find explosives so much quicker than a machine, which didn't have night vision.

The IEDs presented quite a challenge since Rex could find one, but then someone watching could set it off with a cell phone, killing both him and Mike. However, locating an IED and having the team disarm it would save lives of the Americans and the Iraqis. That was their job. They looked out for each other and both were confident, talented and scared. Who wouldn't be? The 2008 movie, *The Hurt Locker*, is also about disarming bombs, but I didn't and won't see it, even though it won six Oscars. I don't think there were any K9 teams in the flick.

After leaving Fallujah, Rex and Mike returned to Mahmoudiyah. On his original visit, he met Suray, an Iraqi translator, and they had many conversations. He was the beneficiary of her family's cuisine – you can just take so many Meals Ready to Eat (MREs). Dowling was separated from Suraj for a while and was anxious to see her again. When he asked another marine about her, he was told that she and her family were murdered for working with the Americans. What a waste of innocent lives that was. Mike wondered why he was in Iraq in the first place.

He and Rex were only to be in Iraq for six months. As they were close to leaving, Sergeant Brian Stokes called on the team for another mission. Then Brian called Mike a not too nice name and was serious in telling him that he was on his way home, first stopping in Al Asad. Stokes left but an IED detonated on top of his vehicle during an attack. Mike wouldn't find all the details until later. The half-year had too many close calls for any K9 team. They were in firefights and saw too much turmoil, but they uncovered IEDs and bomb building materials. They had saved many lives and done well in the country.

He and Rex had been through hell and survived. Only one of them could talk – actually, Rex did communicate with his master in a way very few humans could understand. They cheated death numerous times but put their lives in the other's hands (paws). Rex never got a medal only because working dogs can't receive them in the U. S. military. Today, this amazing German shepherd is still a military working dog in Camp Pendleton. Before that, he went on two more combat deployments.

When Dowling returned home, he made his first stop at Camp Pendleton. He took Rex to his kennel and gave him food and water. Mike removed Rexy's battered collar and made these observations:

> *It is so broken in. I reflect on what it's been through, and what that signifies about Rex and me in Iraq. Our bond is stronger than ever now, man and dog. We know each other in a way that I might never know a fellow human being. Our understanding is instinctive and primeval and it runs so deep.*

Stokes would call him and give him the details about his vehicle and the IED. Brian returned to school, attending Appalachian State. He was an integral part of the football team that won NCAA Division One championships in 2005 and 2006. With the help of Damien Lewis, Dowling wrote about Rex and Iraq in his book of devotion and dependence, *Sergeant Rex: The Unbreakable Bond Between A Marine And His Working Dog.*

The movie, *Ace of Hearts,* is based on a novel of the same name. Ace is the K9 police dog who goes after people who do nasty things, such as steal jewelry and whatever they can find of value in homes. They don't need keys and are the worst example of pop-ins. Ace is smart and doesn't harm the thief, but only holds on to him until he can be apprehended. Usually, he won't even leave teeth marks on the thief, unlike those of Jon Voight, which were left on the arm of Kramer in an episode of Seinfeld.

In the motion picture, Ace is played by not one but two German shepherds – that's how intense the role is. Though the story is fictitious, there are numerous dogs in real life just like Ace – many in law enforcement. Ace winds up being placed on death row for inflicting harm on a person who is actually the villain. I won't give away the ending; if you get a chance, watch the flick, which I think you'll enjoy.

Tommy is a truly amazing seven-year old German shepherd who lives in Italy. For some time he accompanied his master, Maria Margherita Lochi, on errands and to church every day. Sadly, Maria died, but without anyone else leading him, Tommy was at the funeral at Santa Maria Assunta Church in San Donaci. Months after her death, whenever the shepherd hears the church bells chiming, he goes to church, attending Mass. He sits peacefully at the front of the church and doesn't bother anyone. No one complains and parishioners have given him food and water, adopting this devoted dog. Check out the short video at barkpost.com/loyal-dog-goes-to-church.

In November 1941, brick maker Carlo Soriani found an injured dog along the road in Luco di Mugello in Florence, Italy. Carlo brought him home and restored the dog to good health. He and his wife kept the dog and named his Fido, which translated from the Latin meaning *faithful*. Once Fido was OK, he followed Carlo to the central square in town. Later, when Soriani returned from work on the bus, Fido was there to meet him and the two went home. This went on for a couple years, each day.

In December 1943, the area, including the factory where Soriani worked was heavily bombed and Carlo was killed. That day, Fido was at the square but his master didn't get off the bus. The faithful dog went home and for over a decade he went to the square, waiting for Carlo. He did this until the day he died. Many were aware of Fido, with magazines, *Gente* and *Grand Hotel* writing about him. There were several newsreels of the *Istituto Luce* about him. Before his death, the mayor of Borgo San Lorenzo presented a gold medal to Fido in the presence of many town people, including Carlo's widow. A few months before, *Time* magazine had an article on the dog. A four-column front-page article in *La Nazione* was written after Fido's death.

Fido may have copied the behavior and faithfulness from a nineteenth century Skye Terrier named Greyfriars Bobby in Edinburgh, Scotland. Bobby's master was Policeman John Gray, who worked as a night watchman. When Gray died, he was interred in Greyfriars Kirkyard in Edinburgh. Rumor has it that Bobby spent fourteen years guarding his owner's grave, doing this until he died in January 1872.

A few years before, Lord Provost, Sir William Chambers, who was a director of the *Society for the Prevention of Cruelty to Animals* in Scotland, paid the license fee and presented Bobby a collar, which can now be found in the Museum of Edinburgh. You can find a commemoration to the dog in a statue and fountain at the end of the George IV Bridge. Books have been written about Bobby and you can see two movies about him, *Greyfriars Bobby* from 1961 and more recently, *The Adventures of Greyfriars Bobby* of 2006.

Numerous musicians have recorded the song, "Old Blue", including the Dillards, Byrds, Dink Roberts and Pete Seeger. There even seems to be one song of the same name unrelated to canines. Naturally, the ones we're interested in about the dogs that are faithful companions. Many others have performed songs about canines but I don't think Three Dog Night sang any songs about them.

Perhaps the title of the chapter should have been the Lobo song, "Me & you & a dog named Boo." In the canine world, a nine-year old black lab with that name may not have the sight he once possessed, but that doesn't stop him from being a great teacher and healer. He's a therapy animal. He makes a difference around ailing people just by being in the room with them. He is gentle and caring. Young and old feel his presence. Sister Jean, a ninety-four year old resident in Ossining, New York, said very little and couldn't be reached by those around her. That changed when this black lab made an appearance. Sister Jean petted Boo, and before long spoke for the first time in years, uttering the words, *Hello, Boo.*

Youngsters Erich Schneider and Christopher DiSilvio were also greatly changed when Boo entered their lives. Erich was having difficulty brought about mistakes he made – he was close to tears. After a few months he became a changed person with more confidence thanks to our black lab. Christopher had severe attention deficit hyperactivity disorder with a very short attention span. Meeting Boo resulted in his soon being able to sit for an hour without fidgeting. This lab is one wonder dog. He's not the only one.

As reported by Pete Donohue, Erik Badia and Rocco Parascandola of the New York Daily News on December 17, 2013, Cecil Williams, blind and 60 years old, and his guide dog, Orlando, a black 11-year old Labrador retriever, stumbled onto the tracks of the New York subway at the 125th Street platform. The flagman Larmont Smith and others of the Metropolitan Transit Authority shouted to lie down in between the rails, which both man and dog did. Orlando helped Williams scoot beneath an oncoming train. There were minor injuries and Smith commented that a matter of seconds could have resulted in a tragedy. Afterwards Cecil said, *I feel that God, the powers that be, have something in store for me.*

When Williams fell, Orlando stayed with him, when he could have departed. He was even in *St. Luke's Hospital* with Cecil. The guide dog saved his life, which the 60-year old acknowledged. Orlando was unhurt and was called a true hero. Cecil's girlfriend, Cynthia, said: *He's doing great. He's feeling fine. He's resting. He's under observation right now.* Numerous people admitted that they had witnessed a miracle. When this occurred, Williams' insurance would no longer cover Orlando's care costs. As of the summer of 2014, generous people have come forth and Orlando will be able to stay with Cecil. If you'd like to help anyway, Williams said to contribute at guidingeyes.org.

Pransky is a labradoodle, so you can say that she's a French Canadian even though she appears to be Russian. This cross between a Labrador and poodle came about in Australia in 1988, capitalizing on the friendliness of the former and the cleverness of the latter, without the hassles of shedding. Pranksy is cared for by Sue Halpern and the dog's name and the maiden name of Halpern's grandmother are the same. Sue and the labradoodle reside in Ripton, Vermont.

Unfortunately Pransky is not without fault as she sheds, but makes up for that with her intelligence. At times though, Halpern thought the pooch was bored. Sue didn't purchase an iPad for the labradoodle but considered the therapy dog team concept. To obtain certification required passing a test with fifteen tasks. At first Halpern envisioned that as a goal beyond reach. She persisted, accomplishing one step at a time. Two challenges to any dog – both required tasks – were passing by food without salivating and remaining calm in the presence of active children. Eventually certification was obtained for Pransky and the next step was going to the County Home.

In the County Home, Joe was confined to a wheelchair, having had both legs amputated just above the knees. He called to the labradoodle and Pransky sauntered over to him. Joe rubbed her between the ears. Soon Sue and Joe were conversing on canine matters. This scene occurred over and over again as residents would call Pransky by name. Every so often someone might say to Halpern, *Get that dog out of here*, but in more colorful language. More likely people would relate that they had a dog once.

Residents visited by the pooch may have been shy and rarely spoke, but that changed quickly when Pransky pranced into the room. Men and women who had uttered few if any words soon learned the labradoodle's name and beckoned her to come over. This meeting of humans and the canine benefited each of them and Halpern as well. You can read more about this amazing labradoodle in Halpern's remarkable book, *A Dog Walks Into A Nursing Home: Lessons In The Good Life From An Unlikely Teacher.*

I mentioned Rin Tin Tin and we can't overlook Lassie and all the dogs of television. Farfel wasn't one of my favorites because he was a salesman. He sang a commercial for Nestle chocolate from 1953-1965, but should have known better. That stuff can kill dogs. I thought Dreyfuss, played by Bear the dog, was cool even though his name sounded too business-like. He seemed so lovable, gentle and carefree, despite his massiveness. I wouldn't want to pay his food bills, though. Frazier's dog, Eddie, was played by Moose. Don't tell me these canines weren't smart, being featured on so many television shows.

Jenny and John Grogan met in Michigan working on a small newspaper there. They married and moved to the east coast of Florida where he worked for the *Sun-Sentinel* and she wrote for the *Palm Beach Post*. They were married for fifteen months when they thought about the next step. Children were discussed but first the couple figured a pet would be good practice for parenthood. As children each of their families had dogs. Seeing an ad in the newspaper, they drove to a house that had Labrador retriever puppies for sale. They met Lori and Lily, momma of nine puppies. Lily was calm, beautiful and affectionate, impressing the couple.

They decided on a male and one came over to them and convinced them that he was the one. They could pick him up in a few weeks after he had been weaned. John asked where the father was. Lori said, *Sammy Boy? He's around here somewhere.* Jenny and John left and couldn't wait to bring the puppy home. On the way out the door, they saw a flash of something that moved past them and they were reminded of "Wild Thing" that the Troggs sang about. Somehow they felt that they had seen Sammy Boy.

One thing John and Jenny didn't do for their decision was any research on Labradors. Eventually they found out quite a few great characteristics but also that the temperament of both the parents affected the puppies. The soon to be owners of the puppy had a difficult time agreeing on a name. Both enjoyed music by Bob Marley so one day they looked at each other and said, *Marley.* He now had a name but John decided that his full appellation would be *Grogan's Majestic Marley of Churchill,* the road on which they lived.

Labs don't come from Labrador. They were used in Newfoundland for hunting and probably came over from Europe. Known for their intelligence, devotion and gentleness, in addition to loving the water as they dive into rivers and lakes – despite how cold it is – they retrieve game and fish, without devouring their find. In 1990, the Labrador retriever was the nation's most popular breed according to the *American Kennel Club.* In 2004, they retained that position, continuing so for fifteen years.

It wasn't long before John realized that Marley had inherited much from Sammy Boy, the wild lab. He had a mind of his own and ate just about anything in sight, including paper, pencils, sheetrock – he managed his way through the walls – and chewed on furniture and pillows, making a mess and requiring numerous repairs to the house.

Life went on anyway and Jenny became pregnant. After a few weeks, she and her husband went to view the sonogram of the fetus. There was no heartbeat. After further tests, Dr. Sherman confirmed that she had suffered a miscarriage. When they got home, Marley wanted to play but John wasn't in the mood. The son of Sammy Boy went into the living room where Jenny was and put his head on her lap. He was calm and his tail wasn't wagging. She was weeping, but the lab was there to comfort her and remained there for a while.

Soon after the stillbirth, John took Marley shopping and he selected a bouquet of spring flowers for his wife. Stopping afterwards at a pet shop, he bought a chew toy for Marley. He could use it too. Once home, John had a surprise for Jenny as he reached to retrieve the flowers. Unfortunately, the carnations in the arrangement were missing. It's obvious where they were. The *Sun-Sentinel* writer opened the jaw of the lab and found evidence of a carnation. That dog would devour anything.

It was time for obedience school. Maybe that wasn't that great an idea as John had trouble handling the dog with a mind of his own. He disrupted the class and finally the teacher, Miss Dominatrix, decided to show the people how to handle Marley. Her efforts weren't much better than John's. The class broke up and John remained with Marley, but not for detention. She said that perhaps the lab was too young at that point to be trained. In effect, both were booted out of the class.

Jenny and John needed a vacation and the destination was Ireland, where they would spend three weeks without an itinerary. The problem was what to do with the hound, without having to inject a three-week tranquilizer. Finding a babysitter was tough but eventually Kathy, an office worker at the *Sun-Sentinel*, was chosen. She loved dogs and accepted the challenge so John made up an extensive list of instructions. John showed it to Jenny, who asked if he was crazy, saying it would force her to leave the state. Kathy saw the list and accepted anyway. The couple enjoyed the time in Ireland and when they returned home, Kathy was worn-out but surviving. Unfortunately the lab took advantage of her, knowing she wasn't John.

For Jenny's birthday, her husband bought her an eighteen-carat gold necklace and placed it around her neck. She loved it but a few hours later she noticed it was gone. Where do you think it went? Where else? Jenny saw what was hanging in the lab's mouth and they knew. They surrounded him carefully but it was no use as he swallowed it. John figured eventually it would come out so he presented Marley with his favorite fruit, sliced mangoes. John had a routine of checking Marley's deposits, using a stick and a hose. It took a while, but finally it came. Jenny sanitized it and the pair noticed how it shined. They considered a jewelry cleaning service, without revealing the method of cleansing, but that never materialized.

Jenny's second pregnancy was successful when Patrick was born. The concern was how the son of Sam would react. After all, there wasn't much he wouldn't gobble up or at least chew on. He surprised everyone by his love for the boy. The gentle giant would lay down in the nursery with Patrick and became his protector, making sure no one harmed the baby. Jenny thought that he was a devoted canine and would protect her and John against all attackers.

Before Jenny and John moved into their house, there had been a brutal murder right across the street. That wasn't the only one. One night John heard screaming so he rushed out and came upon a seventeen-year old girl who had been stabbed. Others from the area came to help, but they never apprehended the attacker. John calmed her down and waited for the ambulance while Marley was there too, waiting and protecting. Lisa recovered over time and eventually visited John and thanked him. The latter later learned that Lisa had become a television broadcaster.

Jenny's third pregnancy was an ordeal as somewhere around the 21st week she felt that it was time for the hospital. Had the fetus come out, he or she would surely have died. The hospital staff did all they could so she and the child in her womb could make it into the ninth month. Staying in the hospital for a while was followed by being homebound – no lifting, cleaning or anything strenuous. John was responsible for all the household chores, including handling the hound. Aunt Anita came over to help. For Jenny, it was very difficult. On October 10, 1993, Conor Richard Grogan was born.

Despite the joyous event, it took a while before Conor's mother completely recovered from the trying pregnancy. Their canine's continuing bad behavior still frustrated her, but she loved her boys. Instead she took it out on John and Marley, saying to the former that she wanted him out, meaning gone from Churchill Road. A few days later, John thought that her love for Marley returned, but she was of the same mind about the lab.

John decided it was time for more school for the gentle giant. This time it was better as he graduated seventh in his class. That wasn't such a great accomplishment considering there were only eight dogs, but at least he received a diploma, which he ate. John had another task: breaking the dog out of the habit of jumping on people. He got some advice, which mentioned a knee in Marley's rib cage, and it worked, except the master also needed the lab not assaulting others. With the help of his friend, Jim Tolpin, the same method was employed and that was the last time that son of Sammy Boy did that.

With time, Jenny came back and Marley stayed. He even got a part in the movie, *The Last Home Run*, which is listed on the Internet Movie Data Base (IMDB). The flick never made it to the theaters, but Marley is listed in the credits. On the first day of shooting, the dog was uncontrolled, resulting in one take after another. At the end of the day, John was told not to return with the lab. John heard the words: *Don't call us; we'll call you.* Still, he was called and Marley eventually made it to *Blockbuster*.

Thunder and lightning terrified Marley, something that many dogs fear. If he was alone at home and in the garage, he would try to claw his way out. I mentioned the sheet rock before. He made a mess and wound up bloody besides. With Jenny or John around it was better, but still a concern. The same applied to tranquilizers. One day the couple brought home a super cage, made of heavy steel. The family left and felt relieved but on returning home, the lab was staring in the window to greet them. He was a breakaway animal as good as Harry Houdini. They tried locks and other measures, but that didn't stop him. They did more harm as he came up bloody from trying to get out of the cage.

Life went on and John received a job offer with *Organic Gardening*. The family moved to eastern Pennsylvania where the kids would finally see snow. Colleen was the latest addition and youngest, while Marley was the oldest *child*. If you converted dog years to human ones, he was the oldest of the entire clan. He slowed down considerably but still managed his freewheeling ways. His hearing declined and he had difficulty climbing stairs.

101

Then he experienced a bloated stomach and a costly operation was one of the alternatives. There was a very small chance for success with suffering for Marley while the other option was for him to the put to sleep. Miraculously the vet tried a few things and the gentle beast returned home.

At this point Jenny and John saw that his days were numbered and he'd have to face the second alternative. Despite his infirmities, the lab surprised John a few times by his bursts of energy. But then the stomach issue reappeared. John took him back to the vet and knew he couldn't do anything more to save his dear friend. Marley was drugged up and died peacefully. John brought him home and buried him between two cherry trees, which the dog hadn't chewed down. He and Marley had just missed the trees on their toboggan run one winter day.

By now John was writing for the *Philadelphia Inquirer* so he penned a poignant piece on the Grogan family dog. He received hundreds of sympathetic comments through the phone, mail and emails with his news on the world's worse dog. The family was distraught but when people communicated that they had dogs that were worst than Marley in the behavior category, he and Jenny laughed and it soothed them. Marley was devoted, loyal and proof that riches mean nothing. He protected his family and others as well and it didn't matter what religion they professed or what color their skin was. John's dad, Richard Frank Grogan, offered this about the lab: *There will never be another dog like Marley.*

I highly recommend John Grogan's book, *Marley & Me: Life And Love With The World's Worst Dog*, which is a hysterical narrative about love that flowed back and forth in so many ways. There's also a 2008 movie of the same name starring Owen Wilson and Jennifer Anniston. The role of the gentle giant was portrayed by Clyde, Jonah and Rudy.

I've only had three cats for pets – one at a time. They were Jaspurrr, Pearlll and Cricket. Growing up our family had dogs. I remember a few names and something about them, but this goes back a while so my remembrance is fuzzy. Sparky was a toy Manchester. The only thing about him that I recall is that he was small. Mom and dad also had a boxer, whose name escapes me. Then there was Tiger, a Labrador retriever. When he finished doing his thing in the back – not that – it appeared that moles from

Three Mile Island had invaded the area. My father wasn't happy about it at all. Fortunately a woman took Tiger into her care. I think her backyard was concrete.

Then there was a pug named Penny, which is ironic since that breed is very expensive. She had her sleeping facility in the corner of the kitchen and wasn't allowed to move into the living or dining rooms. She knew her place and stayed away, or so we thought. When our family left the house, a small device was put in the doorway so the pug couldn't leave the kitchen. That didn't stop Penny. She hopped over it and headed for the living room couch. As soon as she heard the car entering the driveway, the pooch was back to her bed, as though she had been there the entire time. I wouldn't be a bit surprised if she came back to the kitchen when the car was still on the road. She was one smart canine.

9. White Bird

At one time, the icon for NBC television was a vivid peacock. Actually it was only a slight representation of the bird. The company should have chosen a scarlet macaw, because of its royal blue, black, red, buttercup yellow and green coloration. These birds mate for life, can crack bones with their powerful beak, travel in packs and live for fifty years. Truly spectacular creatures of the parrot family, they are very intelligent, can talk and probably would do well on Jeopardy. Found in Central and South America, scarlet macaws are the national bird of Honduras. You can see a few if you visit Belize.

Not long ago, I read somewhere that the Central American nation on the east coast was a popular vacation destination. A few things found there are creatures that are much more annoying than mosquitoes – they're there too, of course. These flying and crawling things can bite and inject toxins into your body that make your return trip home unnecessary. I won't get into more gross details since people reading this may have already paid for a week there in the coming winter. *The Mosquito Coast*, a 1986 flick, was filmed in Belize. It was one of my least favorite movies even though Sharon was an animal wrangler in it.

That small nation at one time was a British colony that may not be the most corrupt, but it's high on the list of criminal governments and corporations. Fugitives go there to live and not be harassed. For $15,000 to $40,000, you can buy a Belize passport. Many nationals – not commoners – have accounts in the Cayman Islands, are involved in drug payoffs and own yachts. Foreigners who go there in order to make a fortune usually don't succeed, as Belizeans are masters of separating dollars from visitors. When asked what's the best way to leave the nation with a million bucks, the reply is, *Arrive with two*. When election time comes around, the politicos pass out cash, washing machines and hams.

Growing up in Baltimore, Sharon Motola loved nature, training a squirrel to beg at her door for peanuts. He was soon sitting on her knee. Squirrels are rodents, and though that word brings to mind, *vermin*, for her these animals possessed high

105

intelligence. In junior high her pet mouse was Dolly. She won the top prize at a school science fair. Unfortunately, one day Dolly escaped and was devoured by a neighborhood dachshund. After high school, Sharon joined the Air Force and taught male pilots how to survive in the jungle, simulating a plane shot down scenario. She loved camping and the group survived on berries. For the men, it was a struggle. Lizards were the next offering for dinner, which the others avoided. While in the service, she met a dentist, whom she married. He had some good points since he loved nature and camping but wanted children, Sharon had other ideas and after two years she bailed out, hopping on a boxcar and winding up in Florida. She attended a school in Sarasota, studying biology.

Before long, she was working in a circus, taming the tigers. Answering an ad for a Mexican circus, she thought about what that meant: Mexican mushrooms. She was hired but it wasn't exactly what she had in mind. Rocky, a spider monkey, became her friend. Seeing the way animals were treated in the circus, she spoke out and was out of a job. She swam the Rio Grande, with Rocky on her shoulders, and soon hitchhiked back to Sarasota. A letter from documentary filmmaker, Richard Foster, brought her to Belize City. The film was *Selva Verde* and finding animals for the effort was never a concern as so many had been abandoned by their owners: curassows, ocelots and jaguars. When filming was done, Foster left but allowed Sharon to stay at his place, mentioning that she could keep the animals or release them into the wild. She soon started the *Belize Zoo*.

At first, it made no money but she asked for and received contributions, attending many functions to do so. Once she was all muddy and invited to an event. Through a friend Sharon wore a dress made entirely from the woman's curtains, saying, *Scarlett O'Hara, eat your heat out*. I didn't think you could see *The Carol Burnett Show* in Belize. Her zoo was more than an amusement venue. It was intended to serve the animals and teach the people about nature. She hired people who needed work, including Tony Garel, the first employee. The animals were orphans and cripples. The signs were hand-painted and the staff included dreamers and castaways. Sharon was dedicated to the zoo and the locals. She was scheduled to pick up Bruce Barcott at 6 a.m. but arrived at 5.

106

She handed him a cake to hold. It was for the fifth birthday of a staffer's son.

Through a fundraising visit to the United States, Motola encountered officials from the *American Association of Zoological Parks and Aquariums* (AAZPA) who weren't impressed by her. She invited them to visit her zoo, but even then their minds didn't change. She had to speak at the AAZPA conference in Columbus and instead of lecturing, presented a slide show. The officials wanted a first-class zoo in Belize, so she displayed what life was like there. The presentation included views of the hospital as well as the prime minister's home. There were many slides of the poverty of the country. Speaking to the people from AAZPA, she asked, *Does the Beize Zoo exist for these people or the people in power.* The last slide was of a Creole woman enjoying one of Tony Garel's snakes on her shoulders. Sharon concluded by removing her AAZPA badge. *You can have this, because I'm not a member of your organization anymore.*

This wasn't the last time she would face corporate thieves and banana republics. If something wasn't right, she stood up against it. Bruce heard that she could captivate, delight but also frustrate and enrage people, just because she deeply cared for her animals and neighbors. Barcott wanted to meet her and before he did, he asked what he could bring. *Bug repellent*, she replied. The first time they met she told him never to pet a jaguar, even her prize, Angel. She had him go with her for part of the journey, describing the rain forest and all its challenges. Bruce saw her zoo with its 100 animals. It hosted 70,000 visitors a year, being the nation's most visited attraction. Bruce found out about her through the bearded Ari Hershowitz, an organizer of the *Natural Resources Defense Council* (NRDC). Ari helped stop the construction of a salt factory in a lagoon. Now there was new trouble: a dam that would flood the region and wipe out countless animals.

Dams can be found everywhere in the world, supposedly to create energy and provide water to an area. Lately, it has been discovered that these projects aren't that beneficial to people or animals. In many cases they flood a region and deprive natives of badly needed water, not to mention what it does to their homes, livelihood and wild life. The dam was to be built at Challilo on the Macal River, south of the Mollejon dam. Studies were shown –

107

even by the people wanting to build it – that it wouldn't provide many kilowatts of power; would have a devastating effect on the area; actually contribute more pollution, speeding up global warming. The People's United Party (PUP) governed and wanted the dam. The other party, the United Democratic Party (UDP), barely opposed it and only did so because the PUP stood for it. The UDP appeared to be spineless. The project was to be done by a Canadian power company, *Fortis*, along with *Belize Electricity Limited* (BEL). One company, *Dominion Resources*, was also involved, as was *Duke Energy*.

Motola sought as much support and help as she could find, doing studies, looking at other research on the dam, writing articles and speaking for the people and animals. She led the way. Officials weren't happy with her. An announcement came out that a *sanitary landfill* – nice oxymoron – would be built three miles from the zoo. This would mean the end to it. In referring to this project, she called it by its real name: *a dump*. In a letter to Deputy Prime Minister Juan Antonio Briceño, she offered a compromise idea to put the dump near Chan Chich, the extravagant tourist lodge of Barry Bowen. That reply infuriated officials even more. Motola had two thoughts: *damn dump* and *dump the dam*. With time, the dump near the zoo was abandoned.

Sharon and Sho, an associate, saw a wounded young macaw and decided to let nature rule. With time the Zoo Lady changed her mind. The parents would call to the young, who would answer. When Sharon took it under her care, the adult macaws knew that the zoo would help the injured bird. Angel, crocodiles and turtles felt the same way about their caretakers. So did the fish, who knew Sharon by her footfall, which was as revealing as a fingerprint. When Sharon played her guitar and sang, the jaguar was soothed, responding to her playing by raising her paws up.

It was a long struggle and Motola had plenty of support, including Robert Kennedy, Jr., Chris Minty, Ari Hershowitz, the NRDC, zookeepers, journalists, conservation groups, geologists and the people of Belize. These agitators had all the facts and they were right. The government and corporate dam advocates stalled, lied, failed to provide requested documents and treated Sharon as an outsider because she was a *foreigner*. Frustrated, she wondered if it was time to abandon ship. One day a mother and her young son came to the zoo. Motola asked Zeke if he wanted to feed the otter and he was in heaven and said yes. It made his day and somehow affected her as well. Months later the Nesbitts called upon her. Sharon heard the story of the family going to a restaurant in Punta Gorda. Before dinner arrived, their boy went outside to catch some crabs. Two hours later, the lad's body was found as it washed up on shore. His name was Zeke. Sharon had no thoughts of giving up on the dam.

With the dam process dragging on with construction beginning even before approval of the project, Sharon found a new bird: the harpy eagle. The struggle and deception continued but the eco-terrorists won the battle and the dam was dedicated in November 2005. On that day Sharon released into the wild another harpy eagle. Even had she been invited to the dam opening, she wouldn't have gone. Eco-terrorism is a union of regulation ignoring corporations and comatose politicians that pollute the environment, killing wildlife and humans in the process because of their greed. The first definition of the term found on *Wikipedia* is all wrong. Hetch Hetchy was another attempt led by John Muir to halt dam building in Yosemite National Park a century before. It failed but started the environmental movement. Sharon kept it going and was a hero to many, who told her how much they appreciated all her efforts.

Bruce Barcott has many more details about the Zoo Lady and the fight against corruption. His book, *The Last Flight Of The Scarlet Macaw: One Woman's Fight To Save The World's Most Beautiful Bird* is a story of hope, vigilance, politics, conservation, the environment and its connection to people and wildlife. Even when things were bleak, Motola stayed on track, mentioning that there will always be setbacks, but the fight goes on. Even if the conservationists win the battle, there will always be others to go against.

There's another African Grey that needs mentioning. Graycie lives on the east coast and is a wild parrot that probably should have stayed in the rain forest. A resident of Virginia and the DC area, she has resided in a few homes with the least favorite being when she lived in a dark basement. Three children accompanied her with their parents. There are cats and dogs, including a Labrador retriever named Beau. One day he had Graycie in her jaw. Luckily, one of the adults saved her so that Beau didn't have to decide if parrots taste like chicken. I'm getting ahead of myself, so let's go back a few years.

Jenny and Scott knew each other from Penn State University for some time before they began dating. They followed their courtship by marrying. Their first child was Kyle who would later be joined by Kendall and Gillian. Scott's brother Mark gave the couple a present of an African Grey Parrot a few months after their son was born. The new parents soon named the bird Graycie. Mark gave his parents and his sister parrots as well, but Graycie was probably the most rambunctious. Nevertheless, Scott and Jenny were impressed by Barnacle Bill, a parrot they met during a trip to the Caribbean. He could sing at least one song from *The Sound of Music* and was much more entertaining than turning on the television.

From what I wrote about Alex, you know a great deal about Greys. They're intelligent, easily bored and demand almost unending attention. Their claws compare with those of cassowaries and their beaks are strong enough to open Brazil nuts. Pet parrots need their claws filed as well as those powerful beaks. In the wild, nature takes care of that. There aren't more messy eaters and the deposits of parrots are almost impossible to clean up. Jenny was most responsible for this job and figured that except for the green color, parrot poop would make a great grout. Another possibility was using it as glue.

Greys also like to pick on their feathers, creating a bloody scene requiring trips to the vet. They love chewing wood, anything in sight, including people and paper. Anyone who has a Grey doesn't need a shredder. Not only can they talk, they're great impersonators, as I've already mentioned. If you need miscellaneous sounds like lightning, dogs barking and sirens, they can handle that too, enough to drive humans insane. I wonder if Hollywood ever thought of hiring them. African Greys have no trouble sounding like Damien from *The Omen* or Regan from *The Exorcist*. I'm told both of them were entertaining. Once when Scott and Jenny left Kyle with a babysitter, they received a call saying that the baby was fine but she mentioned hearing sounds, *Like there's an angry man in your basement.*

110

When the family grew, Jenny and Scott employed the time-out method of discipline: *That's one. That's two. That's three. Time-out.* One day when this was called for because of the kids, Graycie opened her beak after hearing what was happening and said, *That's one – two! Time-out.* She directed the child to the appropriate corner. Another day a typhoon was on the way to Virginia so Jenny brought the kids and the parrot into the basement. The power went out but the Grey put on a show talking and calming the children. She did come in handy. This wasn't the first time and it wouldn't be the last time the African Grey did her vaudeville thing.

Jenny was always aware of Graycie's being on the attack. Her arms almost resembled that of a junkie from all the beak and claw attacks of the precocious parrot after all she had done for the bird. It surprised Jenny that others didn't face the same agony. Easy going Buddy walked into a room and the Grey seemed to be so friendly to him. She acted the same way with Carolina, a hot Brazilian neighbor and Anne Marie who came from New Zealand. Another charmer was Michael, a friend from the area.

Scott worked at home and used a 3M dispenser from time to time for packaging shipments. Graycie screeched when she heard the sound, but it wasn't long before she sounded just like the 3M gadget as she kept up the noise. There probably wasn't any sound she couldn't copy, including the yelps of puppies. She could drive Jenny crazy from the *plink! plink! plink!* she made with her beak on the bars of her cage. She knew she was annoying her master because she then might say to the dog Bridget, who came on the scene and almost knocked over the Grey, *Bridget! Noooo! You're a bad, bad girl! Stop it now!*

With all her chatter, Graycie became the soundtrack of the family's lives. Years after Beau died, she would mention his name along with the names of other former pets: Hobbes and Mink. At other times she would talk to herself and come up with remarkable thoughts and sayings, even reprimanding herself for her own bad behavior.

Returning to the poop patrol, Jenny guessed that over the course of a year, she went though 180 paper towels. That involved a great number of trees that could have been saved had Graycie stayed in the wild. Doo-doo droppings would have been confined

111

to the rain forest and provided nourishment for the environment. Of course, a bird overhead or a crawling creature may also have devoured her. At times Jenny had thought about making parrot soup in the slow cooker, but then relented. The caretaker heard that African Greys can live to be 80, but a vet offered that he rarely saw parrots in captivity managing beyond the age of 40.

In her book, *Winging It: A Memoir Of Caring For A Vengeful Parrot Who's Determined To Kill Me*, Jenny Gardiner relates much more about Graycie and the Gardiner family, which includes three children and numerous pets. It's a story of love and dedication filled with adventure, frustration and many laughs. I can't recommend it highly enough. If you're thinking about adopting a parrot, be forewarned. It's a great deal of work. You really have to do research and read Jenny's book. Also, if you are still desirous of getting a parrot, procure one from a rescue organization or reputable breeder and not from breeding mills. Gardiner also mentioned *Project Perry* and Matt Smith. It handles all kinds of birds that have been abused or abandoned. Not that long ago they opened an indoor / outdoor sanctuary for African Greys.

The Rev. Henry Ward Beecher offered a quote about crows: *If men had wings and bore black feathers, few of them would be clever enough to be crows.* Half a century ago, a crow lived at the Allee Laboratory of Animal Behavior in Chicago. The bird was fed mash that the keepers moistened. If they forgot, the crow used a plastic cup to do it himself. Otto Koehler cared for a raven named Jacob. Otto had five groups of objects, numbering from two to six along with five different sized boxes in different positions. These had six, five, four, three and two marks on them. Jacob's job was to match the groups with the corresponding boxes. He matched them time after time.

A raven is an oversized crow and both are of the family of *Corvids*, which includes jays, jackdaws, rooks, nutcrackers and magpies. *Corvids* are blamed for stealing crops and eggs from the nests of songbirds. They're also blamed for getting into garbage and leaving a mess. The instances of this behavior are greatly exaggerated. Humans also forget that *Corvids* devour caterpillars, grubs, worms and other harmful pests. Their pursuit of nestlings maintains the health of the songbird family.

Corvids are cunning and adaptable. This flexibility along with the jokester mentality indicates intelligence. Ornithologist John K. Terres posits that of all birds, *Corvids* are the smartest. First place goes to the crow, proclaims naturalist Tony Angell. Writer and zoologist Bernd Heinrich believes that the raven surpasses the crow in this regard and Konrad Lorenz agrees. Those working with mynas and parrots add that their birds can't be ignored. As mentioned earlier, Alex the Grey wasn't the only bird that could talk. Irene Pepperberg compared crows to gorillas and chimps.

According to Aesop – the fable guy – a crow encountered a pitcher with water. There wasn't much inside but the *Corvid* dropped a few pebbles into the container and eventually Charley the crow could drink. After they are born, young pinyon jays can soon recognize their parents' calls. Those that feed only give food to their own, even if a moocher is in the nest. Sorry guy, go to your mom's nest.

Corvids also experience grief. If one loses her mate, noisy visitors will arrive within a few hours to comfort the widow. Catherine Feher Elston's pet crow, Gagee, cared for a wounded fledging. When the latter died, Gagee was silent for four days. If a mate is missing, the other will utter calls to summon the gone bird. Besides bird calls, *Corvids* seem to sprout words. A raven heard explosions that a construction crew set off and answered with, *Three, two, one, kaboom!* Perhaps not as good as African Greys, members of this family can talk and imitate human sounds. After hearing the German word, *komm*, when summoned to eat, a raven uttered that word to another bird to be fed.

Corvids can hide food and then retrieve it, months after they do so. Those that watch may be able to find the nut, but the one who does the hiding just reburies it. Now it's safe from the poacher. Crows and ravens rely on larger animals to kill some of their food supply. Bringing down a deer isn't an easy job. They also hang around eagles just to taunt them. Sometimes that gets hazardous. Those that get away from the eagle or other dangerous animals can survive longer than forty years. You can read more about these amazing birds in the book by Candace Savage, *Bird Brains: The Intelligence Of Crows, Ravens, Magpies, And Jays.*

113

Tibby, a female whooping crane, was brought up by a man from Scotland, who managed despite being on crutches. When the man became seriously ill, he asked Gavin Maxwell to care for Tibby. The guy died, and Tibby wasn't happy, escaping the enclosure that Maxwell provided him. The crane got to the village and seeing a man on crutches, decided to stay with him. The guy chased her away. Soon Maxwell received a call from a person who had seen Tibby and mentioned her acting unusual, trying to follow him indoors. Gavin inquired of the guy if he used crutches and sure enough, he did. The caller was surprised at the reply but Tibby was just connected to a person on crutches who treated her well.

Biologist Marcy Cottrell Houle observed two peregrine falcons, Arthur and Jenny, feeding their young. Jenny left one day, but never returned. Arthur missed her and you could see it by his actions. He called out and when Jenny still didn't appear after three days, he let a cry of despair, filled with sadness. For an entire day he didn't move. Two days later, Arthur left to gather food for the young and was frenetic in his efforts. Nevertheless, three of the five nestlings died, but the others fledged successfully. Arthur's grief is witnessed numerous times in the animal kingdom, whether wildlife or domestic animals.

Sarvey Wildlife Center is located in the state of Washington. It's a place of animal rescue, rehabilitation and release, serving King, Pierce and Snohomish counties. Jeff Guidry heard about it and visited in February 1996. Seeing the cougar, raccoon and owl along with meeting Judy, Kaye and Crazy Bob, he was impressed and put to work that same day. His job was to clean cages and to put the squirrel back when the cage was cleaned. He was successful, but not without some blood coming from his finger. Nonetheless, he would work there one day each week for four hours since he had another job.

On August 12, 1998, *Sarvey* received a new arrival that would change Jeff's life. It was an emaciated female eagle that Crazy Bob brought in. Guidry took her to the vet, after removing the passenger seat of his escort. Now the eagle and driver could see each other. The vet sedated her, took some x-rays and found enough damage to the wings and inserted some pins. On the way back to *Sarvey*, Jeff asked his feathered friend how she felt and assured her that he would take care of her. In time she would be named Freedom.

What was needed was for Freedom to eat. Guidry took care of her and spoke words of comfort and hope to her and she gained weight. Even with the weight gain, she still couldn't stand. She would never be able to fly because of her damaged wings and the decision was made to euthanize her if no progress resulted in seven days. That fatal day that would soon come was a Friday but Jeff only volunteered on Thursday. He went in on his normal day, anyway. When he arrived, the staff was smiling and he noticed that Freedom was standing. Apparently all the talking he did to her paid dividends. Freedom would be used at shows to teach others about wildlife.

Freedom may not have survived without Guidry. Since guests at the rehabilitation center are all rescues, they're also wild. Untrained, uncaring persons wouldn't fit it at Sarvey. Not only that, they'd probably visit a hospital before they resigned from volunteering there. All those humans had something special and the animals related to it. Each respected the other. Some of the rescues didn't survive, just as Freedom almost didn't, but a great number of animals were released into the wild. That was one of the goals.

In spring of 2000, Jeff felt a lump on his neck. It was still there after a few days, so Lynda, his companion, forced him to have it checked out. He had a biopsy and it was determined to be Hodgkin's lymphoma. The surgeon told him his odds were fifty-fifty. When he returned to his family doctor, he decided he needed to go to Virginia Mason because of their oncology center. Lynda mentioned Dr. Andrew Jacobs at Mason. After seeing him, his odds improved, but only slightly. Jacobs informed him it was treatable with chemotherapy. Jeff was still distraught, but was determined to beat the cancer.

There were eight treatments, three weeks apart, so it would be a long battle. Jeff contacted his employer and mentioned his plight to the people at *Sarvey* and received 100% support. Lynda and his family were there for him as well. There were times when Jeff had setbacks, but he learned what he should have done but didn't do. When he felt better, he went in to handle Freedom – I'm sure she knew he was suffering. He had saved the eagle's life so maybe the favor would be returned.

The treatments were done and just after Thanksgiving, he and Lynda went to see Dr. Jacobs. He wasn't at ease – I wouldn't have been either – but things changed when Dr. J. appeared smiling, saying, *You get to live. There are no signs of cancer anywhere.* Jeff and Lynda hugged and soon the doctor had his turn. He also mentioned a drug, Rituxan, which would require four treatments. Guidry agreed to them as well as checkups every three months for a couple years.

When Guidry went back to *Sarvey*, he relayed the good news to Kaye, who herself had battled cancer. He left and took Freedom outside. The air was cold but bothered neither of them, with the eagle on his right arm, facing him. Before long, Freedom could be felt draping over his shoulder with her left wing. She then had her other wing around him so she could touch the center of his back. It was almost like a cape. Being out with her so long, he noticed that this was the first time that Freedom had done that. They looked at each other and the eagle touched his nose gently with her beak.

Jeff was upset with anyone who messed with nature and wildlife. Some dumb guy saw a mother bear carrying her offspring away, leaving another cub, so he took it to *Sarvey*. The mother bear would have returned for the missing cub. As a result, he was at the center in danger of not being released into the wild because of over nurturing. He was raised until he was mature. Fortunately, Jeff noticed that the cub's behavior had changed and it appeared that release could be done. It was successful, something all the staff were happy to see.

There were two other bears involved in the drug trade: Corky and Pumpkin. They weren't dealers or users but victims as they were headed for movie stardom in Hollywood. Their trailer was pulled over and U. S. Customs found marijuana and almost $200,000 cash. Corky and Pumpkin were delivered to the center, but they were full-grown, so ease into the wild wasn't an option. They weren't that healthy either but the staff remedied that. Next was to find a place for them. Selected was the *Wild Animal Orphanage* (WAO) in San Antonio. Corky and Pumpkin had a new home with a few other bears. They all spent evenings playing

Bingo. Seriously, when Jeff later visited WAO, Corky recognized him and lowered her paw. She almost seemed to say to him, *Hey, I've missed you. And thanks.*

Guidry wrote a book about *Sarvey* and his experiences, but needed an ending. What he wrote in the last chapter was as good as the rest of the book. Over time, people think they can make a wild animal a pet. It's not meant to be, so don't do it. Stick with a dog, cat or pet rock. Another annoying observation of Jeff is that building condominiums and businesses leave animals with no habitat, or one that's toxic. I've read his book and highly recommend it. Its title is *An Eagle Named Freedom: My True Story Of A Remarkable Friendship.* After further consideration, I believe I chose the right title for my book.

I'm not sure how Ben Franklin would have felt about Freedom – the bird not the other concept. I'll deal with that shortly. The turkey on your Thanksgiving table evolved from wild turkeys. The name probably originated because the British made an association between the bird and the country of the same name. Domesticated turkeys don't fly but the wild ones can for about a quarter mile, despite their size. They wind up in trees, although not in the stands of the hunters, I don't think. Besides the familiar gobble, they emit putts, cutts, whines, kee-kees, and clucks. All these sounds have meaning to other turkeys, some as warning others and as mating calls. I'm sure one represents a reminder that football on Thanksgiving is coming soon. Turkeys eat grasses, trees, shrubs, nuts, berries and insects. Sometimes they consume small reptiles and even visit bird feeders.

Predators of turkey eggs include raccoons, skunks, foxes, groundhogs and rodents. The young and adults have to watch out for coyotes, wolves, bears, hawks, eagles and humans, who are at the top of the list. Nonetheless, turkeys are fighters, using their beaks and legs against those after them. They can also run or fly away, chasing humans as well as four legged attackers. Over two centuries ago, Benjamin Franklin preferred the turkey to the eagle as the national bird. He felt that the latter was of bad moral character, not obtaining his living in an honest way.

Violinist David LaFlamme wrote and produced the song "White Bird" in 1969 for the musical group, It's a Beautiful Day. David sang it with Pappi Santos. The song was over six minutes long but shortened for airplay, reaching the number three spot on San Francisco station KYA. Sadly, Santos died twenty years later in a car accident.

10. Fly like a Beagle

The title of the chapter is from a 1976 song by Steve Miller and his band. It reached the number two spot on the Billboard Top 100 the next year. Excuse me, I'm told that the smash hit was actually "Fly like an Eagle," but this chapter is about more dogs so the beagle stays. It's certainly appropriate for Charles Shultz's Snoopy. He may be a figment of the cartoonist's imagination, but that beagle did his share of soaring.

Though this treatise is about animals, I must talk about Dick Wolfsie first. That's appropriate because of his surname. In school, he was a class clown, always ready with a humorous reply. He spent detention time for it, but students laughed and so did teachers – some anyway. He graduated from New Rochelle High School and followed that up with a degree from George Washington University. Seeking a job after graduation, he returned to the high school. The secretary asked if he was the same guy who graduated from the school four years ago and he replied in the affirmative. He was interviewed and they hired him anyway. He taught psychology and English and was successful because students learned while he was entertaining.

He eventually worked in New York and Chicago for a few television stations, ending up at *WISH-TV* in Indianapolis. He met Steve Allen and Art Buchwald. Appearing on *Good Morning, New York*, when Allen was talking about Stan Laurel, he asked, *Where can you find people of that ilk anymore?* Dick responded, *You could join the Ilks Club.* Steve laughed. Meeting Buchwald and presenting him some of his work, Art looked at it, wrote a few words on one of the papers and Dick departed. Later he read what the humorist had written: *Wolfsie, stay out of my racket.*

Over the years, Dick had worked at numerous jobs, but Indianapolis seemed most suited to his liking. It even got better one morning when he left for work. Departing the house, he spotted two eyes. They weren't that of a leprechaun, but belonging to a beagle, who seemed to be saying, *please.* He was trapped so he put the dog, whom he soon named Barney after a character on the *Andy Griffith Show*, into his home. He left for work and figured he'd see Barney later. Little did he know how much damage the beagle could do.

Barney would eat anything – he was a true omnivore. He wouldn't completely devour tables and chairs, but certainly did a lot of chewing. Mary Ellen, Wolfsie's wife, didn't hate dogs, but this pooch seemed to change her mind about them. During the time the television guy was away, Barney couldn't stay inside the house because of the limitations of the Wolfsie's home insurance policy. Tying him up outside would only result in his howling endlessly, which didn't thrill the neighbors. So Dick took him to work – not for Barney to find a job, but to remain in the car. The barking continued. The beagle was also a great escape artist as he could open the window and leap out. Soon Dick brought him into the studio. Dick would take him on mornings when he was on assignment somewhere.

The duo had quite a few adventures, including an incident when Barney lifted his leg on a small television set showing sports reporter Vince Walsh doing an update. This was outdoors. Dick was called to see Paul Karpowitz, the general manager of *WISH-TV*. It certainly didn't look good. Inside the office, Paul asked Wolfsie, *Did you think that was funny the way the dog urinated on the TV monitor?* Dick didn't reply, but many others laughed and so did he. Karpowitz then assured Wolfsie that he thought it was hysterical. Some time after this, Barney's bladder wasn't empty as he did justice to a rival station's sign.

From that point, it was all gravy for the duo. Rin Tin Tin and Lassie may have rehearsed and had to do retakes, but not the beagle. It came naturally and *WISH-TV* wanted it no other way. Barney went to obedience school but didn't get much out of it, except a certificate. Wolfsie felt training him would spoil the spontaneity. Dick's show had many viewers and Barney his fans. Even Mary Ellen came around to love Barney – almost. At least she didn't divorce Dick. Their son, Brett, wasn't a big fan of his antics but somehow got along with the beagle without feeding him chocolate.

Soon, the beautiful beagle was on magnets, tee shirts and men's underwear. He graced the cover of *Indianapolis Monthly* three times, three more than Wolfsie. He wasn't any threat to Siskel and Ebert but reviewed movies thanks to *Barney's Bad*

Movies, a late night talk show. Karpowicz came up an idea to show bad old movies and have the hound give a thumbs up or thumbs down, something he couldn't do since he slept through them – even *Lassie Come Home*. Dick and Barney visited schools and children loved them, the latter replying with all kinds of mail. Fans sent in pictures they drew and paintings they made of the dog. Wolfsie's favorite was art from barbed wire. Bill Arnold made a life size image that was both uncanny and realistic. People sent so much stuff that Mary Ellen took some for the living room and the rest went into the basement.

An idea came to name a drink after him at Ruth's *Chris*, a steakhouse chain. Named after Ruth Fertel, Barney and his master visited her, emphasizing the dog's food choices. Ruth wasn't concerned. Barney took off and returned with a 40-ounce chunk of meat, which Ruth didn't make much of a fuss about. The station manager nixed the idea of the Barney drink and Dick felt a non-alcoholic drink might work. When the manager left and was replaced, the program went ahead with the drink. Viewers chose the winner, which was comprised of cranberry juice, vanilla flavoring, club soda and a twist of lemon: *Barney's All Bark, No Bite.*

The TV canine showed his feelings many times and didn't lose his appetite. You already know about the 40-ounce steak he procured and showed his master. When four sticks of butter went missing, guess who was responsible? Paula Dean would have been proud. Once, Barney roamed from home and did some shopping – without a cart. Dick was notified that Barney had been arrested. Someone went to buy some milk and saw the famous beagle coming down one of the aisles with a barbequed chicken. It wasn't wrapped and didn't have to be. Even if the food was hidden, you couldn't keep him away from it.

Despite his food cravings, Barney was loyal to his master and a smart dog. On one of the morning shows, Dick's guest was a Bill Clinton impersonator, Damien Mason. Mason sat in one chair, Wolfsie in another and Barney in the third one. Damien went on lampooning Clinton and finally looked at the beagle and said, *Barney, I'm not happy with Al Gore. How about being with me on the ticket as vice president?* Dick's dog shook his head, departed the chair and headed out the door. One other time a band started to

121

play some Mexican music – they were so bad they wouldn't have passed the audition for *America's Got Talent*. Barney went to the outlet and withdrew the cord. He had a snack at the same time.

Barney was quite a dog. You can read all about him and his master in Wolfsie's book, *Mornings with Barney: The True Story Of An Extraordinary Beagle*. Just like the people of Indianapolis, you'll delight in the beagle as well as Dick's story.

There are more stories about beagles, which I'll get to. For now, it should be noted that dogs have wolves for relatives, since canines evolved from those wild beasts. Just compare a wolf, *Canis lupus*, with a German shepherd and you should see the similarity. Even the scientific names are almost identical. Werewolves aren't part of the family, even as cousins somewhat removed.

In the city of Buffalo lives Annie the beagle. She lives with my sister Pat and her husband, Lou, and the canine's full name is *Annie Rose Petunia Nose*. If given the chance, Annie will chase any bunny rabbit she sees and probably won't gather in the hare, but if the beagle is in the house and spots a rabbit – or even senses that one is nearby – she'll howl. I'm not sure what Annie would do if she lands her prey, but I wouldn't put money on the rabbit.

As far as culinary choices, this beagle just could be an omnivore. She loves corn and can't wait until the fresh corn arrives. She's not too happy in August when she isn't presented a cob of corn to demolish. She likes blueberries and beer, too, but not together. In early 2014, Pat left some hummus and bābā ghannūj in a bag and she and Lou left the house. Each dish was in a sealed plastic container. Annie found no obstacle, opening each dish and indulging. If she had been able to speak, she probably would have offered compliments to the chef. Lou and Pat are both great cooks. This might explain why the beagle is a dumpster diver. Really, she just got into the garbage receptacle in the kitchen one day. That didn't last long as the homeowners figured out a way to lock her out. It doesn't mean she won't return to her diving.

As most dogs, Annie can sniff out food in another county. That's a great exaggeration, but a canine's aroma seeking ability is forty times that of people and may approach being one hundred times greater. Bloodhounds are the leaders in this category. This explains the devouring of the hummus and baba ganush – another of many spellings – but Annie also found candy they shouldn't have, especially chocolate. The wrong kind can result in a dog becoming sick or even dieing. The safest kind is white chocolate, while baking and semi-sweet chocolate are the worse. The culprit is theobromine, which is poisonous to canines. Annie's latest chocolate caper happened around Easter of 2014. Somehow a small candy rabbit – I think both ears were missing – was in the proximity of the beagle. It didn't take long for her to proceed. She didn't devour the base since it was too thick. Her reward was getting slightly sick afterwards.

Annie is a loving animal who gives love while receiving it. When Pat and Lou head out on vacation, my niece, Liz, and I beagle sit. Liz does most of it and when either of us departs, Annie howls – barking in sadness – unlike the cries of happiness she sends forth when we arrive at her home. She is one intelligent canine bringing joy.

What follows next is the story of Jon and Maria and their dogs: labs, border collies and a rottweiler-shepherd mix. Each loves dogs but were going through tough times as both their marriages were crumbling. They lived in Upstate New York not far from Albany. Maria was a frustrated artist who spent time remodeling houses with her then husband. She adopted her dog and named her Frieda, because of her eyebrows, which brought to mind the Mexican artist, Frieda Kahlo, who was also referred to as Frida. Maria got the canine from the rescue center because she figured no one wanted a dog that was both German shepherd and rottweiler. She was right on the money in that assessment. Frieda had been treated badly by her owners and spent a year at the shelter. The dog and her new owner loved, respected and cared for the other.

Caring for canines, Jon Katz sold books on dogs that he wrote and worked to save old barns from being demolished, not an easy task. For one barn, he thought a window or two would be a great addition. He went over to look at some and met Maria and the ferocious Frieda. One was a delight to him while the other female overwhelmed him with her barking. At least no blood flowed. Talking with Maria, he realized that she didn't really discipline the dog, whose life had been so tough that the task would have been difficult for anyone.

Jon found it easy to talk to Maria and she liked Jon as well. Each was still married so they settled on being good friends. Occasionally they would have lunch or dinner together, although Maria always insisted on either splitting the cost or paying for it the next time. Each still faced tough times and relied on each other. Eventually, Jon was divorced and Maria was waiting for hers, which later came. The real problem was that Jon couldn't come between Frieda and Maria. The dog writer came up with the beef jerky solution, which he would try with Frieda. He dropped it off for her and then repeated that the next day. Jon knew he had to be patient. The same could be said of his relationship with Maria, who wanted to prove that she could survive on her own.

Besides Maria, Frieda didn't care for people or other dogs. Jon knew this and kept his distance. It appeared that matters were improving when on one occasion Jon got a call from a director of a nursing home, asking for Izzy, the writer's border collie. There was a food fight and the proprietor didn't want to call the police, fearing some arrests. Izzy and his master made the trip and soon the residents began petting Izzy, terminating the tossing turmoil. Coming home, Maria was coming down the driveway with Frieda, dragging her along. When the two dogs were close, Frieda was raging, but Izzy ignored her, behaving as if Maria's protector wasn't there. There was no contact between the canines and Frieda must have been puzzled and certainly affected by the encounter.

There was another similar encounter between Frieda and Lenore, the black lab who was about three years old. The two dogs were close to each other when Lenore fell to the ground. Then Lenore licked Frieda's nose and did it again. The rottweiler-shepherd was confused but soon she sniffed Lenore, whose tail was wagging during this time. Jon suggested the four of them stroll along together, which they did without incident. This illustrated that there was hope for Frieda. Lenore was a huge influence in Jon's life, making him aware that love was still a part of it, sustaining him.

Katz lived each day being patient with Frieda and her master. He knew that the dog had been treated badly, but needed to find out more. He posted a picture of the canine on his blog, asking anyone who knew anything about her to contact him. He heard from Stella in the nearby town of South Glens Falls, who thought she knew her – the Kahlo connection may have been a clue. She felt that her husband, Steve had obtained Frieda from a breeder to protect his auto business at night, which had been robbed a few times. The dog was confined to a kennel all day and then let out at night to patrol a gated area. Once out of the kennel, Steve and others would antagonize Frieda, poking her with sticks and tossing rocks at her. Soon kids in the neighborhood were doing the same thing.

When Jon drove over to see Stella, she felt guilty about this horrible treatment of Frieda, whom they called Brownie, but she really couldn't stop it. She was glad that the dog was in a better home and asked Jon if she could see her. Quickly he replied it wasn't a good idea. Then Stella mentioned the night Brownie was howling, louder than usual. She was aware of a house on fire and only through her loud barking was a neighbor's family rescued even though the house wasn't. However, insurance provided the funds to rebuild the dwelling.

Jon learned that Brownie dug a tunnel and escaped but returned on the fifth day. It was soon discovered that Brownie would soon be a mother. Steve couldn't handle that so one day he drove the dog into the Adirondacks and abandoned her. Most dogs wouldn't have survived that ordeal, but Brownie accepted the challenge. She found food and shelter, gave birth and the puppies soon left on their own. Eventually students at Adirondack Community College became aware of her, calling her ACC, the acronym for the school, located north of Glens Falls. Because of what Brownie had been through, she was hard to pin down. However, she wound up at the *Queensbury SPCA*.

Katz learned a lot about Maria's dog, but became more enlightened when he returned to see Stella, this time bringing Frieda (or ACC or Brownie). He changed his mind about bringing Frieda after some thought. Before seeing her, he met Cheryl, who knew of the dog, whom the family called Goldie. It's no wonder this pooch had problems. It didn't take long before Jon asked her: *This was the house with the fire, right?* Indeed it was. Cheryl affirmed that she had saved their lives, including her son Sean. The lad had a great relationship with Goldie, bringing her food and treats. Jon wondered what wrong had been done to the dog.

125

Katz would then see Stella and she got a glimpse of Frieda, but it was only a small one before she closed the door and went inside. Jon had one more stop to make at the breeder's place. The latter wasn't very friendly and the writer saw an environment that wasn't too clean or welcoming. Jon was happy to leave the place and had enough information to understand what Frieda had been through.

Winters being as brutal as they were in upstate New York, Maria and Jon knew they had to be someplace warmer, even if for only a few days. Jon loved *Disney World*. When someone advised him to go to a warmer place, Jon said, *I can't afford it*. His therapist replied, *You can't afford not to*. Jon set it up. At first Maria was doubtful, but after a few days in Orlando, she loved the place. They met people and told them of their love and they received great support. This bolstered their self-esteem and the short stay in Florida played a huge role in future events on the farm.

They returned home and Jon had some ideas, based on his knowledge on what Frieda had been through: the actions of the breeder and Steve, especially the desertion of the pregnant dog in the Adirondacks. One day Jon heard a big commotion and went to investigate. Inside the gate of her compound, Frieda was sitting on a large deer. Katz uttered, *Frieda, get off that deer*. She did and the deer left the area. The dog listened to him and would keep doing that.

There were times when Frieda took off and didn't return for days. When she did, she was bloody and bruised. Eventually she stayed on the farm, abandoning that behavior. When she first came to the farm, she wanted to chase every moving creature: dogs, cats, chickens and other farm animals. She soon became their protector. Frieda had watched over Maria, but now she had the same concern for Katz.

Jon's book, *The Second-chance Dog: A Love Story*, relates more about himself, Maria, Frieda and animals on the farm. Watch the video of Frieda at http://www.bedlamfarm.com/?s=FREIDA. Another web site is fullmoonfiberart.com. Jon had asked Maria Wulf to marry him numerous times and she finally agreed to do so on June 12, 2010. The ceremony was performed in the barn and the only missing creature was Frieda, whom Maria felt should be kept away because of all the people. Katz and a wulf can live together in harmony.

The puppy had been beaten to the point of death when he arrived at the *Ardmore Animal Hospital*. He was in such bad shape that the emergency room doctor was going to send him to the *SPCA*, where his life would be terminated. When hospital administrator Diane Klein came in and saw him, he was missing his left ear and part of his face. Diane's dog Maddie had died two years before from cancer. Her mission was to save the dog. Exactly what had happened was unclear, but another dog or some person could have done the damage. It may have involved dogs tearing at each other, but he was so young he certainly wasn't doing any battling. Later it was learned that he was bait in dog fighting.

Diane called Dr. James Bianco for his input but he thought the case was hopeless and the best choice was for him to be euthanized. Diane pleaded and the doctor agreed to try surgery. It took several hours but was a success, but only the beginning. The young pit bull must have suffered immensely, but all those in the hospital noted that he wasn't whimpering or showing any sign of what he should have been experiencing. He must have had a high level of tolerance for pain. He was progressing, but wasn't eating. Bianco opened his jaw and saw why as he removed a half-dollar sized piece of the puppy's jawbone. With it inside, it had been so painful that the dog couldn't operate his mouth. Before long his appetite was back.

He stayed in the hospital for ten days and then Diane took him home for rest and recovery. Because he was white and reassembled a cotton ball, she named him Eli, after the inventor. She would have loved to keep him but there was a jealous dog in her home so her work was to get him ready for adoption.

Larry and Jennifer married and were set on having children but nothing seemed to work, finally deciding on adopting. One place refused to work with them because Larry was over 40. The non-profit organization *Golden Cradle*, founded by Arty Elgart, was more accommodating. Elgart had to wait five years for the child he and his wife were blessed with. One thing that Arty said to the waiting couples was: *I want you all to relax. You're all going to be parents.*

One Saturday morning the phone rang. The voice on the line said, *This is the stork calling.* They waited two years but their first son came with a bonus. Larry and Jennifer named the twin boys, only three days old, Noah and Dan. The couple had bought nothing in the way of baby stuff, so they had to buy all the necessities for the two right away. The separated the babies by color: red for Noah and blue for Dan. The couple didn't see much sleep the first half of the year, but they didn't mind, being overwhelmed with joy. As Dan and Noah grew, they learned they were adopted but accepted that very well.

Shortly after the twins celebrated their twelfth birthday, the family cat Buzzy wasn't feeling well. Larry and the boys went to *Ardmore Hospital* and left him overnight. Before they departed, a member of the staff brought a white puppy on a leash. He warmed to Dan and Noah and as they bend over to pet him. The puppy licked both their faces and Larry picked him up, cradled him and soon his face was being kissed. He was one happy dog. The little white creature was Eli with the missing ear and left side of his face. Before long the Levins knew the story of the beaten pit bull.

They lost fourteen-year old Buzzy but adopted the white puppy. Jennifer was reluctant but on seeing Eli and with Dr. Bianco's convincing words that the puppy was so friendly and wouldn't harm a soul, she accepted him into their home as their third adoptee. Larry considered a name for him. The young dog certainly was ugly but you couldn't call him that so he figured why not Oogly, which was close, settling on Oogy.

Oogy was similar to dogs that chewed on everything in sight, but the family loved and protected him. They replaced the old dilapidated electric fence with a new one and Larry got him accustomed to it. Because of his missing ear, the teacher figured Oogy might be confused as to where the buzz was coming from and would run past the fence. He consulted with a company representative and soon Larry sight-trained Oogy, solving the problem.

After seeing pictures of Bud the famous pit bull, I wasn't convinced that Oogy was of the same breed. Larry was told that those dogs didn't get bigger than 50 pounds, but Oogy surpassed that very fast. When the puppy was taken to *Ardmore* for his six-month checkup, technician Karen saw the dog and said, *That's a*

Dogo. At the end of the session, Levin took out his credit card but was told that Oogy was a no-pay dog – the dog's owners wouldn't ever have to pay for any surgery at *Ardmore*. What Diane, Doctor Bianco, the staff at *Ardmore* and the Levin family had done for Oogy just showed how unselfish and kind they really were.

Larry did some research and found that from the pictures Oogy wasn't a pit ball at all. Dogos are also called Argentine mastiffs and they're hunting dogs, but not like retrievers. They hunt puma and boar and can kill their prey. Dogos are lively, gentle, fearless, smell detectors and they are huge dogs – having the traits of Great Danes.

The Levin dog had four more surgeries, including one for his face since he was still in pain. It helped. He was limping around due to a tear in his anterior cruciate ligament and had surgery for it. The same thing happened to the other leg and there was more surgery. Oogy wasn't thrilled about water therapy so an alternative was found. All in all he accepted everything well, buoyed by the love showered on him.

The Levin family loved Oogy and he returned that love. Any friends or relatives of the family loved and were loved by the Dogo. When people saw the dog, they stayed away, not because he was a pit bull, since he wasn't, but because of his face, all thanks to what happened to him as a puppy. Eventually those in the neighborhood petted him and asked for his history, which Larry, Jennifer, Noah or Dan related. Walking down the street with his master, Oogy looked like a senator running for office. Oogy barked at other dogs and people, but only because he wanted them to play or slobber them with kisses. Maybe Larry should have named him *Lickity Spit*. One of the Dogo's most joyful moments was frolicking with other canines.

People were inspired by the dog, especially individuals who had gone through tough times. After knowing what he had suffered and miraculously survived, they were convinced that they could conquer any adversity. He set a great example and his love helped the others immensely.

Larry Levin wrote about Oogy and his family in his book, *Oogy: The Dog Only A Family Could Love*, which begins with the horror of dog fights and ends in the two-way love between family,

Oogy and the *Ardmore* staff. I think the title should have been *Oogy: The Dog That So Many Loved.*

11. Butterfly

Like many animals, bats have gotten a bad reputation. Maybe the blood connection has something to do with that, but people should pick on larger creatures. Contrary to some opinion, they aren't blind. They're nocturnal and one of very few mammals that fly. Since bats leave the cave at night for food and don't have night vision goggles, doing so in the pitch black poses great challenges, so they must have truly keen senses. One thing they are blessed with echolocation, a type of sonar. Dolphins also use echolocation and their use of it matches that of bats. Also adopting it are swiftlets from Southeast Asia, oilbirds of South America and some humans.

Bats send out a signal and another comes back. They can distinguish between the two waves and thus avoid smashing into walls. I don't know how they capture mosquitoes, but if they're intelligent enough with the sonar stuff, they won't go hungry. Female bats that are nursing consume twice their weight in food or more each day. Males and the other females eat about half their weight. They all digest food quickly, requiring plenty of nourishment. Their diet consists mostly of insects, plants and nectar. Some eat frogs, but are smart enough to avoid the deadly arrowhead ones. Some of them are fruit eating bats. Many devour arthropods – spiders, krill and fiddler crabs. A few bats prey on fish and indulge.

Besides echolocation, bats also use heat detection and smell. They have quite a few tools for moving around at night. Bats are great contributors to the environment. They devour various types of insects – I've already mentioned mosquitoes – without which picnics would be fraught with pests. We could bring out the repellent or resort to bug zappers, but chemicals do harm to the earth and humans. Zappers don't discriminate, killing beneficial insects and even small birds. Ridding an area of some of the mosquito population may also prevent the spread of viral diseases such as encephalitis and West Nile virus. Fruit eating bats help by dispersing seeds, which can later provide more fruit. Bats aren't evil, but an essential part of the ecosystem. Besides caves, they live in trees, bat houses and even the homes of some people.

They have the ability to squeeze through very narrow openings. That may be why they're in your attic.

The blue morpho is another designation for the blue butterfly. A 2004 movie that I highly recommend is *La Mariposa Azul*, whose title translates to the name of that species. Starring William Hurt as Alan Osborne, it is the story of Pete Carlton, a ten-year old boy diagnosed with cancer. One of his wishes is to go to the rain forest to find the blue morpho. After hearing Osborne talk, he tries to convince the scientist to take him to the rain forest. Alan mentions that it may be too late in the year, as well as the fact that he doesn't handle children very well.

Eventually, Alan, Pete and his mother, Teresa, embark on Pete's dream. The movie is a magical journey of hope and redemption, and you'll have to watch it to see if they find the blue morpho. *La Mariposa Azul* is based on a true story, and it might change your life.

In the early twenty first century, I noticed a beautiful flying lime-green creature resting on the front of my house. It was a Luna moth, which has a wingspan of almost five inches, making it one of the largest North American moths. Butterflies and moths both belong to the order *Lepidoptera*, but the latter is nocturnal, while butterflies thrive in the daytime and are larger and more colorful. The covering of the pupa of the butterfly is a chrysalis while that of the moth is a cocoon. These are some of the differences.

When I lived downstate, I had to put up with devouring gypsy moth caterpillars, who could make a summer oak tree appear to be a winter one. If you sat out on your deck or porch and these critters were in branches above you, blessings above would shower down on you and you'd have to shower or at least change your clothes. You might be able to stop their advance up the trunk of the trees by circling it with some grease mechanism. Fortunately the caterpillars weren't around every year, but that could easily change.

I encountered a friendlier and more helpful invasion not that long ago when my sunroom was filled with ladybugs. These flying insects are a thorn in the sides of aphids, who love roses. Years before that day, I had some roses, but they didn't survive. I transported the ladybugs outside via my vacuum cleaner and they were free to get rid of other pests. Some bugs look like ladybugs.

132

These imposters are called Asian lady beetles and they may do more harm than good.

Plants and pollinators need each other. Without the latter, many plants just couldn't survive and vice versa. Pollinators gather nectar from the plants and in turn allow for growth of plants. Pollinators include bats, bees, flies, wasps, butterflies, moths, beetles, ants and birds, especially hummingbirds, honeyeaters and sunbirds. These aren't the only pollinators, without which humans would find food hard to come by. Men, women and children may be able to live with the fruits of *better living through chemistry*, but that effort has failed miserably when it comes to flavor and good health. Genetically Modified Organisms aren't good for anyone. I should add these words to the four in italics: *but not for long*.

Besides performing essential work, pollinators are extremely intelligent. Just consider some of migrations of birds. They don't all travel from the arctic to the tropics and back every year, but many manage to fly enormous distances without getting lost. *Winged migration*, a 2001 documentary covering four years, follows the migration of birds traveling hundreds of miles to warmer climates in the fall and then back to cooler places each spring. To reach their goal, they use no special compass, only that of nature and the stars. Flying over water poses problems finding food, but somehow they manage.

More recently, a PBS program featured a six part series called, *Earthflight*. Airing in September of 2013, the journey covered Africa, Europe, South America, North America, Asia and Australia. Using sophisticated technology with cameras mounted on the fliers, the views gave us a breathtaking bird's-eye view of the trips – what did you expect? Once more these birds can only be described as amazing.

Even more incredible are hummingbirds, that I mentioned earlier, who have to consume enormous amounts of food. To travel across the Gulf of Mexico takes about twenty hours. Maybe they swoop down for seafood, but I doubt it. How do they survive for almost a day without any food? They also find their way on their own and without any *American Automobile Association* maps. I think the right word to describe this migration is miraculous.

As incredible as these small birds are, there are smaller creatures that are more impressive. Because of the cold winters, monarch butterflies move south to Mexico or friendlier places, weather-wise, in the United States. They are the only insects who migrate each year to a warmer climate 2,500 miles away. They do this because of the food they need. Monarchs survive on milkweed plants and also get nutrients from flowers. They have to return in the spring for the same reason. The migration starts in October of each year, but might begin sooner if the cold hits ahead of schedule. On arrival, they hibernate in the same place every year, even though they are not the same butterflies.

Early in the year, monarch butterflies depart hibernation and search for a mate. After this is done, they lay their eggs on milkweed in March or April. In less than a week, larvae or caterpillars will appear. The caterpillars will be full-grown adults in two weeks, soon entering the Chrysalis stage. Then the butterfly appears, living only two to six weeks, but will repeat the process to create another butterfly. In all there will be four stages of monarchs, but the last is the one that will migrate. It will survive from six to eight months. All in all, a monarch can live from two weeks to eight months.

Many of the pollinators may not be to your liking, but that doesn't mean they aren't necessary in the big picture. A few creatures are hated, some even feared. As you know, most animals move out of your way and will only respond if you threaten them or their family. I can't say I blame them. Besides what has already been mentioned, the hate list includes bees, worms, ants, scorpions, mosquitoes, hornets, wasps and snakes, who feed on small rodents – another not so likeable group. Those slimy crawling animals have been known to devour small deer. They can skip breakfast, lunch and dinner for quite a few days. Specifically, a rattlesnake can swallow a mouse in September, crawl into his den for the winter and manage without a meal until the following June. Alan Boone inquired of Mojave Dan – more on these two later – about why rattlesnakes don't bother Native Americans. There seemed to be a gentlemen's agreement between them. It had to do with respect and attitude. Native Americans have no fear of crawling creatures and don't set out to massacre any snake they see. White people seemed set on killing every kind of snake, not just rattlers.

Spiders freak people out but they devour many bugs that we'd rather not see around. For those with arachnophobia, you'll be assured to know that an acre of land has about 80,000 spiders. Most animals, whether loved or hated, are integral in the role of prey or predator, the former being someone's lunch and the latter ridding the area of pests.

People usually freak out when an ant or two is found in their abode. One day Allen Boone saw a few families of these tiny creatures in his kitchen and on the porch – maybe it was an entire nation. Boone talked to them saying he wasn't sure they belonged in his home. He was nice about it although he did mention his ability to banish them all very quickly. He was calm and understanding of them in his talk. He left to go to a comedy theater. When he returned, all traces of the ants were nowhere to be found. Since that time, those tiny, industrious creatures have never bothered him.

As far as scorpions go, they all have venom but only about three percent of those creatures possess deadly poisons for humans. This species goes back more than 400,000 years. They feed on insects and their eggs, spiders, termites, small snakes, lizards and rodents. On the Internet, you can find a list of what to feed your pet scorpion. What would we do without the World Wide Web? If you're still not relieved, you can move to Antarctica, where they can't be found – yet.

You may not want to read the next two paragraphs if you're about to have dinner, especially if it's spaghetti and meatballs. Scientists have found that there were fewer allergies with people having worms in their bodies. It's weird, makes one cringe and I have one word for it: *yuck!* I saw this revelation in the summer of 2014 on the CBC program, *The Nature of Things*. Fortunately David Suzuki and others felt that there was a better alternative. If a child was allergic to peanuts, small amounts were presented and gradually increased over time, under strict supervision. This worked in many cases and a child who avoided peanuts started to like them and not have side effects. This gradual method pleased many people as opposed to the crawling choice.

Worms do have their place. Putting them on a hook before fishing may not be what kids or adults relish doing, but the results could be a nice sized bass or yellow pike. If you have a compost pile in your backyard, you can tell how rich the mixture is by the size of the worms. Without those creatures, you'd have to drive to the farm store for compost. They can inhabit a pile of dirt, newspapers, weeds, grass clippings, fruit and vegetable waste and make it truly productive growing vegetables. Better still, worms can perform the same magic on a pile of garbage. Maybe it contains the remains of some fancy dining.

Most species – including worms – play a huge role in the environment since one that is endangered is so necessary for other plants and animals. When it is extinct, a domino effect begins. It might take a while, but soon other species disappear, forever. Homo sapiens is as much a part of the ecosystem as weeds, vegetables, trees, deer and fish of the sea. It's the idea of interconnectivity, which implies a link between two objects, going in both directions.

Consider the rain forest and the macaw, a creature that is so beautiful and colorful that individuals want to capture it and sell it for huge profits. In the process, as is expected, many of the birds die, which happens when they can't adjust to living inside someone's home, away from their natural habitat. In the forest they find nourishment, but what they're looking for isn't all that abundant. They seek out a special kind of nut, enclosed by a rock-hard shell. Even with a hammer, humans will find it extremely difficult to open, unless they have dynamite. The macaw uses its strong beak and finds the task relatively easy. In the process of opening the nut, some of the fruit falls to the ground or water below. This excess is enjoyed by other creatures nearby, which in turn may become prey for larger animals. All these small events keep the system flowing and in harmony.

Another example is the tapir, that won't win any beauty contest unless the judge is Mr. Magoo. This creature thrives on fruit from the forest. With so much fiber, the tapir lets go of some body waste after indulging. The area is blessed with organic compost and seeds from the fruit. The latter is helpful in replanting another tree, which eventually produces more fruit. Human hunting affects the tapir, the seeds and the rain forest – another example of interconnectivity.

For the longest time, many scientists believed that animals weren't smart, weren't capable of feeling emotions or couldn't figure things out. In some circles, neurologists and other specialists looked down on podiatrists and doctors of internal medicine. There was the same discrimination as *regular* doctors were regarded as superior to veterinarians. In this last slighting, when someone asked, *What do you call a physician?* The answer was, *A veterinarian who can only treat one species.* Veterinarians are neurologists, oncologists, dentists and family physicians as well. Moreover, today getting into veterinary school is harder than being accepted to med school.

It's common knowledge that animals have cancer – leukemia, melanoma, for starters – just like humans. There are no reasons why DVMs couldn't share information about the disease with oncologists and vice versa. The same applies to other health issues such as heart attacks and digestive issues. Between the medicine of humans and animals, there's no dividing line and never was or should there ever be. In 2007, Roger Mahr and Ron Davis met in Lansing, Michigan, discussing their professions. The former was a veterinarian and Ron a physician. They discussed cancer, the problems of smoking, viruses and diabetes. More importantly, they asked for the end of segregation between their two professions. By working together, the health of humans and animals could be improved. When Jerry's friend Kramer went to see a vet for his nasty cough, he was on to something. And yet, we laughed. There aren't many books that I've written without a mention of that show.

Zoobiquity is the term that writers use for a more inclusive approach to health care, combining the treatment and healing of patients of all species. B. Natterson-Horowitz and Kathryn Bowers combined to write the book, *Zoobiquity: What Animals Can Teach Us About Health And The Science Of Healing.* Barbara is a cardiology professor at the University of California at Los Angeles. Kathryn writes for *The Atlantic* and teaches a medical course at UCLA.

"Butterfly" is the name of a tune by Swing Out Sister, made up of Corinne Drewery and Andy Connell. Originally comprising three members, they chose the name because it was the only one they agreed upon – they all hated it. Released in 2008 on the CD, *Beautiful Mess*, I hadn't heard the song until the summer of 2014.

12. The lion sleeps tonight

Massage therapy has been around for centuries – for animals as well as humans – even though it has only been realized as important in the United States for less than two decades. Shortly after Anthony Guglielmo opened his office for human massage, he received a call to look at a horse named Champ, who'd been abused. Since animals weren't his stock and trade, he said no, but Sylvia said she'd call back in a few days. Tony did some checking and before long was on his way to a horse massage instruction session.

It was ten hours away in Ohio. After a week, he had massaged five horses and learned a great deal in the process. He came home, called Sylvia and said he'd look at Champ. His experience paid off and Sylvia was impressed with Guglielmo. Tony even survived being in the same place with Cocoa, who recently had surgery and probably should have been avoided. Tony made some contact with the horse and avoided being booted out of the facility.

He and his wife Cathy visited the Florida Keys for a vacation and stopped at the *Dolphin Research Center*. Like bats, dolphins use echolocation to determine the size, density and shape of objects close to them. Tony saw a few of these creatures including Cindy, who was unlike the others. She was thin and in need of something, so Lynne, the medical director asked him for help. Since he and Cathy were about to end their vacation, Lynne figured that Tony needed a week to familiarize himself with the ailing dolphin. Arriving at home, Guglielmo checked into some east coast aquariums about dolphin massage, but had no luck. When he called the *New York Aquarium* he was told that there was an animal there that he could look at. He now had a bigger challenge.

Nuka was an 1800-pound female walrus having health problems. That was what she should have tipped the scales at but only managed to be 1300 pounds. Her hips and rear flippers weren't functioning properly and that contributed to the difficulties. However, Tony began some message therapy. After a few weeks, he came to see her at the aquarium and spotting a walrus, didn't think it was Nuka, as her hips were normal and she was using her flippers the right way. Guglielmo had worked his magic again.

As expected, the *New York Aquarium* had some Atlantic bottlenose dolphins and Tony massaged two of them, Tab and Presley. Since boys will be boys, they were troublemakers. Guglielmo had to soothe them out of their aggressive habits. He had more luck with Tab than his buddy but knew that working with them would give him experience that he needed for handling Cindy. After a few sessions, Presley was still being a rascal until Tab appeared next to him and it appeared they were having a conference. From that point on Elvis was more cooperative, indicating that Tab had told him to knock it off.

When Tony first saw Rudy the penguin, he thought he was looking at Quasimodo from the Victor Hugo novel. When he moved closer, the therapist hadn't encountered such a horrible odor. They looked so adorable in the *March of the Penguins*. Tony would have to breath through his nose for a while. Guglielmo started in on Rudy, who was less than a foot tall. His second massage was a week later and Tony noticed that Rudy had really grown. His posture was improved as well. The penguin would get bigger and have ten weeks of treatments. Once again, Tony's method worked, even though Rudy still had a slight curve in her back – it took a while, as is the case with all penguins – but Rudy was found to be a female.

Guglielmo had another walrus to tend to. Wanda was lethargic and obviously suffering. She wouldn't eat, either. She was scheduled for an endoscopy except that the vet administering it wasn't big on alternative medicine. Tony was summoned before the procedure to see what he could do. Though in pain, Wanda knew that Guglielmo and the others were friends in the area to help her get better, so she was submissive. The master was at it but trying a few things didn't help. They had to change strategy. Then Wanda became so relaxed that she had a small bowel movement. The group knew that Wanda would make it. The endoscopy that followed revealed a plastic bag and handball inside the walrus. After returning from the hospital, the other walruses greeted her and were happy to have her back.

Maybe massaging a shark isn't a great idea and hasn't been done – that is, until Tony met Baby the sand-tiger shark. Sadly, sharks have a bad reputation, unjustly so. Blame it on the movie, *Jaws*. You may not have noticed then when humans are attacked by these creatures, it's because the latter thinks they found a sea lion, which unlike the two-legged victim, tastes like chicken. Maybe that's not true, but sharks really don't like the way humans taste. I won't go any further with that.

Gugliemo worked on Baby, but carefully. She was so named because she was the smallest of the litter. After messaging for almost forty minutes, the shark relaxed and Tony found what he thought was an air bubble between the skin and the muscles. It certainly would explain Baby's behavior. A stethoscope and ultrasound confirmed that the masseuse was correct. A week later Dr. Paluch, the aquarium veterinarian, used a long needle to get rid of the bubble. At most other aquariums, Baby would have been euthanized, instead of being given a chance. This was thanks to Tony and the others.

Guglielmo has massaged more than a hundred animals comprising seventeen different species. Besides those mentioned, he also worked on these creatures: Mambo point, a trotter, who returned to his winning ways with his master and rider, Mike Sorentino, Jr.; a boxer named Reddog – a canine not a pugilist; Mickey, a seventeen year old striped cat; a supposedly defective ferret – that's quite common; Kathy, a Beluga whale; Cindy, the dolphin mentioned earlier; Snuggles, a long-eared bunny. No doubt, these creatures are similar to humans, since each has emotions and feelings. Suffering reaches both species and massage can offer great relief. You can read more in the book by Anthony Guglielmo and Cari Lynn, *The Walrus on My Table: Touching True Stories of Animal Healing.* Obviously animals are smarter than many people think.

Far away in Nairobi, Kenya, can be found a rescue facility, the *David Sheldrick Wildlife Trust.* In 1974, a baby elephant needed more than just nourishment. Daphne Sheldrick became the foster parent, but feeding Aisha a variation of cows milk didn't help. Aisha was still sickly. Other liquids were tried with no better results. It wasn't until coconut milk was given to her that the baby elephant's health improved. Aisha followed Daphne around as if the latter were her mom.

Aisha was still quite young but she was doing fine. One day Daphne had to fly to her daughter's wedding, leaving the young elephant. There were others who would take over her role. Soon, the young elephant wouldn't eat and with each day, became worse. By the time that Daphne returned, Aisha was nothing like she had been before Daphne departed. She soon died. Aisha had suffered *sudden-death syndrome*, *broken-heart syndrome* or *gripping fear*. Staff members were grief stricken, none more than Daphne. It was like losing a child. The story of Aisha and Daphne was first aired on the PBS's *My Wild Affair* on July 16, 2014.

I mentioned the naturalist and author Jeffrey Masson earlier. In 1987 he was visiting a game preserve in India when he came upon a few elephants. When he was about twenty feet from them, a large elephant flapped his ears. Jeffrey answered with *Bhob, gajendra*, an elephant greeting. The animal let out a roar, which Masson felt was a friendly retort. It wasn't and the initial ear movement was a warning. The pachyderm charged him and he tried to run away, realizing that elephants can outrun humans. Eventually, Jeffrey tripped and fell into some tall grass, which saved him since these animals have bad vision. It was a close call and he was lucky.

Indeed, elephants, like many animals, have feelings such as joy, sadness, compassion and happiness. They can feel pain and suffer. Game warden G. G. Rushby was doing some elephant control as he shot a few females, but wounded a small male. He was dazed and not sure what to do when the orphaned calves came to his rescue, helping him and leading him to safety.

In the southern part of Kenya is a region called the Amboseli. Wildlife thrives there and for over 400 years so did the Maasai tribe, being great protectors of the land. They didn't hunt the animals but protected them from predators. In 1974, Amboseli National Park was created and the Maasai were asked to depart. The tribe was given some compensation and still reside close by, treating the animals well, for the most part.

The park is home to numerous herds of elephants. In September 1978, a project was initiated to study them. Led by Cynthia Moss and Martyn Colbeck, the team set up tents and noted the behavior and habits of these massive animals. At times they watched from their Land Rover, with a few of the species calmly approaching and accepting of the scientists. They also came close to the area of the tents to feed. They were a fearless and friendly bunch of creatures. Humans and pachyderms showed great respect for one another.

Elephants in the Amboseli live together in families, led by a matriarch. At age fourteen, males typically leave the group so families consist mostly of females: the leader, daughters, granddaughters, cousins and aunts. One such clan is the EB group, headed by Echo, who was initially joined by Erin, Emily, Eudora, Ella and Little Male. Naturally, in time, others joined the group. Echo wasn't responsible for the naming. Cynthia, Martyn and other researchers did that, but after being called a name, an individual elephant identified with it.

Echo, who led the EB members for over nineteen years, was given her name based on the sounds emulating from her collar. Observing elephants, Cynthia's team noticed that they were very emotional and devoted to the members of the herd. When Emily died, her bones were found and Eleanor, Edgar and Erin knew that they belonged to Emily. In general, watch over the dead covered a few days – such was their concern and feeling. When Grace gave birth to a calf that died hours afterwards, she and her older calves were distraught.

The only concerns of the observers were males who could become aggressive at times. Elephants were concerned about predators, but were safe inside the park. They roamed outside it during the dry seasons and then were in danger from poachers seeking ivory. In October 1989, all international ivory trade was banned. Another affect of the dry seasons was the birth cycle of calves, which was delayed because of the condition of both the females and males. A lack of nutrients produced lethargic elephants.

EB members accepted the scientists and trusted them, but they had stronger bonds within their family. As you may have guessed, elephants are smart animals with feelings. Some can live to the age of 60 or 70. Average weight of an African elephant is from two to six tons. The Asian variety weighs less. A calf is walking almost at birth. There are numerous videos and nature programs about these amazing animals. You can read about them in the book by Cynthia Moss and Martyn Colbeck, *Echo Of The Elephants: The Story Of An Elephant Family*.

A week after the sad story of Aisha, *My Wild Affair* featured the story of Chantek, an orangutan brought up as a human child. Lyn Miles was a graduate student in Chattanooga at the *University of Tennessee* (UT) in the late 1970s and her project was to communicate with Chantek, who was only a few months old. This was through sign language. The orangutan is the fourth species of great apes and Chantek wore diapers, but he learned quickly, even providing some signs of his own. As might be expected, one was for eating, which he mastered after a month. He called ketchup *toothpaste* and bottled water to him was *car water*. Working with the orangutan was more than a full time job for Lyn, but student volunteers helped her. Ann Southcombe played a huge role as a full time caregiver and teacher.

Chantek rode in the car to fast food places. He didn't drive probably because Lyn and Ann hid the keys and he didn't know about hot wiring. He loved orange sherbet – after all, he was an orangutan – and pistachio ice cream, preferring it from *Dairy Queen*. He also loved cheeseburgers. He was into the business world and knew the value of cash, more or less. When he asked Ann for a drink, she would sign, *Where's your money?* He'd give some to her. Real coins were used at first and then washers. He may not have been that smart – on second thought, maybe he didn't know about counterfeiting.

If the orangutan wanted to head out for some ice cream, he'd point Ann to her car. Then he took the keys and opened the door and they were off. He knew the way there, too. Chantek was extremely intelligent. He knew how to work with tools – more on that shortly. He rode a tricycle and helped cleaning up, which he didn't seem to mind. If he followed Lyn out the door, he observed and then could escape by himself.

As he matured he grew stronger, similar to that of a half dozen men or more. A full grown of his type could weigh 200 pounds. Just like Christopher Hogwood and Stoffel, you couldn't keep this orangutan penned up. He was so smart he unraveled the meshing in a chain link fence, left and then restored it so you couldn't tell how he got out. A fence with some electric didn't fool him. He used a small stick to short it out and then left without needing a comb to straighten his hair. He returned to his trailer with soda and sweets, but he could have hurt himself as well as others. The university was concerned and then it became an issue when a co-ed was attacked. She had no serious injuries, but before long the orangutan was banished from the program, after being on campus for eight years. It wasn't because he hadn't graduated.

Chantek wound up in the place from which he came, the *Yerkes Natural Primates Research Center*. He wasn't happy in a five by five cage, from which he couldn't escape. Depressed as he was, he managed for eleven years. In 1997, he then was moved to the *Atlanta Zoo*, a place he liked better – anyplace had to be better. It wasn't the UT, but the zoo is known for the largest collection of orangutans in the United States. Once the orangutan left UT, Ann and Lyn visited many times. Once he asked Miles for ice cream and a whopper, but she knew how he felt when he was gently told no.

For quite some time, he thought of himself as an *orangutan person*. Chantek did have other orangutans at the zoo, so he had some companions. He called the caretakers there, *key men* since they carried the keys wherever they went. Today, Chantek is 36 years old, thriving and has a girl friend orangutan. You may wonder where the orangutan went when he slipped away at night from his trailer. One clue may that he never got a university degree. Second, like humans, he was smart and didn't need it. Chantek wasn't about to look for a job.

You can watch the video about Chantek, Ann and Lyn at video.pbs.org/video/2365286726/?start=60. You can also visit the orangutan's website – I told you he was brilliant – at Chantek.org. Actually it's Lyn Miles' doing about her work. *My passionate and life-long commitment is to see Chantek and other enculturated apes as persons living in culture-bearing communities, with agency and choice.* – H. Lyn Miles

Chantek wasn't the only animal in his species that had deep feelings. Washoe was a chimp that gave birth to a baby that died a few hours after because of a defective heart. Her second baby, Sequoyah was sickly and perished at the age of two months from pneumonia. Researchers brought Loulis, a ten-month old chimpanzee for Washoe. At first it appeared that Washoe wouldn't accept Loulis but that changed. The chimp became a dedicated mother, with Loulis learning over four-dozen signs from her new *mom.*

From so many of these animals, what I have read and written in this book should convince you that many scientists have it all wrong when stating that animals aren't intelligent. In most cases, they haven't done the research. As Aisha and Echo illustrated, animals have intense feelings. They experience joy, sadness, despair, loneliness and disappointment. Like Alex and Graycie, they can say, *I'm sorry.* They're clever, as Chantek proved by his night moves and even more so by his chain link fence restoration. Did you forget that he could use tools and brooms to clean up, just like Felix – Unger, not the cat. Christopher Hogwood could leave the premises too and he was loved and returned that love. He had to be smart to escape becoming ribs or sausage.

Some might insist that humans can't be matched because of language, but dogs, cats, lions and birds communicate with other animals in their family as well as with other species. It's just in a language that many people can't comprehend. That shouldn't surprise us since many humans speak only one language, and that one not very well. Though animals fight and we know about predators and prey, when it comes to WMD and all-out war, wildlife, domestic and captive species are superior to humans, *hands down.* Maybe, that should be *hands up.*

Androcles and the lion

In Rome, people gathered to watch the Great Circus, where beasts battled slaves. The master of Androcles was an ex-consul and the latter cringed when he saw his opposition: a huge lion. As the animal slowly approached Androcles, he was terrified. But the animal was wagging his tail and soon licked the hands and feet of the slave. The two recognized each other and Androcles was relieved. Later Caligula asked Androcles why his life had been spared that day. The slave related the time he escaped to a cave and a large lion entered it, but he was wounded. The man removed a splinter from the lion's foot and treated the

146

injured paw, which the lion placed in Androcles' hand. He then went to sleep. They lived in the cave for three years with the lion hunting for the pair. Androcles was recaptured and then condemned to death in the arena. Because of this day at the Great Circus, the people voted for freedom for both Androcles and the lion. 'This is the lion that was a man's friend; this is the man who was a physician to a lion.'

"The Lion Sleeps Tonight" is a song also known as "Wimoweh", "Mbube", "Azimbawe" and "Wimba Way". Many artists have recorded it but the Tokens had the biggest success when it rose to the top of the charts in 1961, earning over fifteen million dollars in royalties. A few lines from it follow.

In the jungle
The mighty jungle
The lion sleeps tonight
In the jungle
The quiet jungle
The lion sleeps tonight

The king of the jungle and his friends are at rest there – it's their home. Sadly, humanity has messed up the picture, starting with the endless massacre of species as already pointed out. The animals' homes have been decimated by the destruction of the rain forest and building of developments. When trees are leveled and the area turned into farmland, the result is the same. Wild animals captured for collectors of exotic pets have a difficult time in their new environment. Many die on their way out of the jungle. Anyway you look at it, this is poaching. No one should have cobras, panthers, wolverines, honey badgers, scorpions, spiders or giraffes for pets.

When it comes to having a dog or cat as a *family* member, caution should be exercised. African Grey Parrots are easily bored so they need constant attention. Sheepdogs are used for herding other animals, and since they love to run, living in an apartment in the city will not be to their liking. Even not so active dogs want company, which is hard to provide in this crazy 24/7 world. Before you get a pet, do quite a bit of research and thinking.

13. Bless the Beasts and the Children

"Bless the Beasts and the Children" is a song written and performed by Karen and Richard Carpenter in 1971 for the documentary with a very similar title. It's about poaching and I haven't seen it. Most likely I won't watch it. Killing animals for tusks or anything else is abominable and a huge threat to the planet.

You may have heard of Strongheart, the work dog, war dog and Hollywood star. He was a German shepherd whose real name was Etzel von Oeringen. His movies include *The Silent Call*, *North Star* and *White Fang*, all from the 1920s. He came before and led the way for Rin Tin Tin. When both filmmakers Larry Trimble and Jane Murfin were needed in New York, Allen Boone was called on to dog sit. The deliverer of the dog spoke to Strongheart with intelligence just as he would to a smart person. Boone was willing to have the shepherd stay with him. The dog entered the house and moved from room to room like a building inspector. Then he went outside to do the same. When he finished, he gently licked one of Boone's hands, in approval.

At night Strongheart was on the bed with his head near Boone's head. When asked to turn around, he did, but then wound up as before. Allen found out that Strongheart, reacting to various sounds, did this to protect his temporary keeper. The dog understood Boone more than Allen did Strongheart, but the former realized that he could pick up signals and know what the shepherd wanted. The canine had toys to amuse himself that he would get from the closet and then return them there when he was finished playing. He also came around to help Allen in what he was doing.

Boone had a relaxed schedule each day. Strongheart changed that by demanding Allen rise at six a.m. Retiring for the night at a certain time was ruled by the dog too. One day Allen asked himself if he should finish writing or head for the mountains with the canine. He decided on the latter but so did Strongheart, without consultation. Just as animals can understand and respond to what humans are saying, Allan found that Strongheart would know what was on Boone's mind even if his *boss* hadn't opened

149

his mouth. Allan was told that this was a natural instinct that most dogs possessed.

When a visitor appeared at the house one day, Strongheart didn't eat him but wasn't very friendly to the guy who was on a mission for magazines to write articles on the dog. The shepherd fangs were flying and the visitor was glad he was wearing brown pants. The next day, Allan discovered the guy wasn't a writer after all but a dog trainer out to see what made Strongheart such a great movie star. A similar response happened in Los Angeles when Boone met with his friend and his associates. Strongheart didn't like one of the people, who turned out to be a dishonest promoter and was later indicted.

When Allan left Strongheart home alone, on his returning the dog anticipated his arrival. In fact when Allan decided to leave his work place, the shepherd stopped what he doing – dog stuff – and moved to his observation spot. Mohave Dan, the *desert rat*, told Allan:

There's facts about dogs and there's opinions about them. The dogs have the facts, and the humans have the opinions. If you want facts about a dog, always get them straight from the dog. If you want opinions, get them from a human.

Strongheart died on June 24, 1929 at the age of eleven. I've mentioned Boone earlier relative to ants, rattlesnakes and skunks. You can read about his amazing encounters with animals in his mid twentieth century book, *Kindred With All Life*.

Brian Hare is an animal scientist who has done numerous studies on many species of animals. Along with his wife, Vanessa Woods, he wrote the book, *The Genius Of Dogs: How Dogs Are Smarter Than You Think*. It sheds a great deal of light on animal intelligence, even though the title might suggest that the book concentrates only on man's best friend. Hare's book discussed many scientific trials that he and his wife conducted.

Former psychoanalyst Jeffrey Moussaieff Masson has written more than a dozen books on animals. The title of his 400 page book, *Altruistic Armadillos, Zenlike Zebras: A Menagerie Of 100 Favorite Animals* gives you a good idea of what's inside. Writing about four pages on each, Masson informs and amazes readers with just how smart these creatures are. He talks about animals that aren't so familiar to us: bilby; bonobo; cochineal; echinna; kakapo; dugongs; okapi; pinnipeds; tuatara; yeti. Jeffrey mentions the myths and then sets the record straight as best as possible. In some cases, not enough research has been done so he admits that he and others just don't know about a creature. At the back of the book, he lists alphabetically – but only three books for each animal – more references and reading suggestions.

Do animals have as much intelligence as people? Many scientists say *no* because of communication. Not only did Strongheart listen to the individual that delivered him to Boone, he also understood him and responded. Dogs and many other animals manage that with barking and body language. It's up to humans to understand the conversation and continue in it. If the licking of Boone's hand by Strongheart doesn't convince you of the dog's smarts, I hope that the other animals I've mentioned result in a change of heart.

Like humans, flying creatures and those with four legs have limitations. However, outside of pigeons, they don't drop bombs on hospitals, nursing homes or on innocent people. They don't wage war against other nations using nuclear weapons. Animals don't own homes with 10,000 square feet or more and rely on fossil fuels for the utilities. They don't take more out of the earth than they put in. Animals are like the Native Americans who take only what they can use and put back more into the ecosystem that they remove.

The animals in this and the previous chapters are all heroes. So are their caretakers. Together, they're inspirational as well. Animals are intelligent, reasoning, emotional and above all loving, caring and faithful servants. Once in a while they may not like a person, but this feeling is justified. Even after a dog leaves a present for his master and hears about it – it's not an anniversary, Christmas or a birthday – Fido forgives and continues in his devotion. This love is unconditional, just like that shown by God for his children, who fail at times.

Speaking of the Creator, a bible passage in the book of Genesis says man should have *domination over every creeping creature that moveth upon the earth*. Obviously, many people misunderstood this last command. Either that or the translation

151

wasn't quite right. As far as we know, God created the animals first and then man. Science tells us that humans followed the dinosaurs and the other creatures. This order is true whether you're a creationist or an evolutionist – some people are both. What follows is a reading list. One book I should mention is the one co-authored by John Lloyd and John Mitchinson, *The Book Of Animal Ignorance: Everything You Think You Know Is Wrong*. Please give your pets the love and respect they deserve.

References

Anahareo – *Devil In Deerskins: My Life With Grey Owl* (1972: New Press)

Bruce Barcott – *The Last Flight Of The Scarlet Macaw: One Woman's Fight To Save The World's Most Beautiful Bird* (2008: Random House)

Mark Bittner – *The Wild Parrots Of Telegraph Hill: A Love Story – With Wings* (2004: Three Rivers Press)

Andrew Blechman – *Pigeons: The Fascinating Saga Of The World's Most Revered And Reviled Bird* (2006: Grove Press)

J. Allan Boone – *Kinship With All Life* (1954: Harper & Row)

T. Coraghessan Boyle – *A Friend Of The Earth* (2000: Viking)

Anthony Bourke and John Rendall – *A Lion Called Christian: The True Story Of The Remarkable Bond Between Two Friends And A Lion* (1972: Doubleday)

Lilian Jackson Braun – *The Cat Who Talked Turkey* (2004: Thorndike Press)

John A. Byers – *Built For Speed: A Year In The Life Of Pronghorn* (2003: Harvard University Press)

Rachel Carson – *Silent Spring* (1962: Houghton Mifflin)

Kevin Clash – *My Life As A Furry Red Monster: What Being Elmo Has Taught Me About Life, Love, And Laughing Out Loud* (2006: Broadway Books)

Vicki Croke – *The Lady And The Panda: The True Adventures Of The First American Explorer To Bring Back China's Most Exotic Animal* (2005: Random House)

Rachel D'Oro – *Dog Praised For Helping Save Owner's Home* (April 25, 2010 – Associated Press)

David Dosa – *Making Rounds With Oscar: The Extraordinary Gift Of An Ordinary Cat* (2010: Hyperion)

Mike C. Dowling and Damien Lewis – *Sergeant Rex: The Unbreakable Bond Between A Marine And His Working Dog* (2011: Atria Books)

Nicholas Evans – *The Horse Whisperer* (1995: Delacorte Press)

Jenny Gardiner – *Winging It: A Memoir Of Caring For A Vengeful Parrot Who's Determined To Kill Me* (2010: Gallery Books)

Meg Greene – *Jane Goodall: A Biography* (2008: Prometheus Books)

John Grogan – *Marley & Me: Life And Love With The World's Worst Dog* (2006: William Morrow)

Sara Gruen – *Water For Elephants: A Novel* (2007: Algonquin Books)

Anthony Guglielmo and Cari Lynn – *The Walrus On My Table: Touching True Stories Of Animal Healing* (2000: St. Martin's Press)

Jeff Guidry – *An Eagle Named Freedom: My True Story Of A Remarkable Friendship* (2010: William Morrow)

Sue Halpern – *A Dog Walks Into A Nursing Home: Lessons In The Good Life From An Unlikely Teacher* (2013: Riverhead Books)

Brian Hare and Vanessa Woods – *The Genius Of Dogs: How Dogs Are Smarter Than You Think* (2013: A Plume book)

Bernd Heinrich – *The Snoring Bird: My Family's Journey Through A Century Of Biology* (2007: Ecco)

Laura Hillenbrand – *Seabiscuit: An American Legend* (2001: Random House)

Philip Hoare – *The Whale: In Search Of The Giants Of The Sea* (2010: Ecco)

Don Höglund – *Nobody's Horses: The Dramatic Rescue Of The Wild Herd Of White Sands* (2006: Free Press)

Wendy Holden – *Haatchi & Little B: The Inspiring True Story Of One Boy And His Dog* (2014: Thomas Dunne Books)

Mark W. Holdren – *The Raven* (2007: Powell Hill Press)

Mark W. Holdren – *Spirit Wolf* (2004: Powell Hill Press)

Glynnis Hood – *The Beaver Manifesto* (2011: Rocky Mountain Books)

Seth Kantner – *Shopping For Porcupine: A Life In Arctic Alaska* (2008: Milkweed Editions)

Jon Katz – *The Second-chance Dog: A Love Story* (2013: Ballantine Books)

Barbara Kingsolver – *The Poisonwood Bible: A Novel* (2005: Harper Perennial)

Peter Laufer – *The Dangerous World Of Butterflies: The Startling Subculture Of Criminals, Collectors, And Conservationists* (2009: Lyons Press)

Larry Levin – *Oogy: The Dog Only A Family Could Love* (2010: Grand Central Pub)

Sharon Levy – *Once & Future Giants: What Ice Age Extinctions Tell About The Fate Of Earth's Largest Animals* (2011: Oxford University Press)

John Lloyd and John Mitchinson – *The Book Of Animal Ignorance: Everything You Think You Know Is Wrong* (2007: Harmony Books)

Yann Martel – *Life Of Pi: A Novel* (2003: Harcourt)

Jeff Moussaieff Masson – *Altruistic Armadillos, Zenlike Zebras: A Menagerie Of 100 Favorite Animals* (2006: Ballantine Books)

Jeff Moussaieff Masson and Susan McCarthy – *When Elephants Weep: The Emotional Lives Of Animals* (1995: Delacorte Press)

James A. Michener – *Creatures of the Kingdom* (1993: Random House)

Sy Montgomery – *Birdology: Adventures With A Pack Of Hens, A Peck Of Pigeons, Cantankerous Crows, Fierce Falcons, Hip Hop Parrots, Baby Hummingbirds, And One Murderously Big Living Dinosaur* (2010: Free Press)

Sy Montgomery – *The Good Good Pig: The Extraordinary Life Of Christopher Hogwood* (2006: Ballantine Books)

Cynthia Moss and Martyn Colbeck – *Echo Of The Elephants: The Story Of An Elephant Family* (1992: William Morrow)

Farley Mowat – *Never Cry Wolf* (2001: Back Bay Books)

Vicki Myron and Bret Witter – *Dewey: A Small-town Library Cat Who Touched The World* (2008: Grand Central Pub.)

Vicki Myron and Bret Witter – *Dewey's Nine Lives: The Legacy Of The Small-town Library Cat Who Inspired Millions* (2010: Dutton)

William Nack – *Secretariat* (2010: Hyperion)

Barbara Natterson-Horowitz and Kathryn Bowers – *Zoobiquity: What Animals Can Teach Us About Health And The Science Of Healing* (2012: Alfred A. Knopf)

Stacey O'Brien – *Wesley The Owl: The Remarkable Love Story Of An Owl And His Girl* (2008: Free Press)

Mark Obmascik – *The Big Year: A Tale Of Man, Nature, And Fowl Obsession* (2004: Free Press)

Naomi Oreskes and Erik M. Conway – *Merchants Of Doubt: How A Handful Of Scientists Obscured The Truth On Issues From Tobacco Smoke To Global Warming* (2010: Bloomsbury Press)

Susan Orlean – *Rin Tin Tin: The Life And The Legend* (2011: Thorndike Press)

Irene Pepperberg – *Alex & Me: How A Scientist And A Parrot Discovered A Hidden World Of Animal Intelligence – And Formed A Deep Bond In The Process* (2008: Collins)

Glenn Plaskin – *Katie: Up & Down The Hall: The True Story Of How One Dog Turned Five Neighbors Into A Family* (2010: Center Street)

Monty Roberts – *The Man Who Listens To Horses: The Story Of A Real-Life Horse Whisperer* (1997: Random House)

Candace Sherk Savage – *Bird Brains: The Intelligence Of Crows, Ravens, Magpies, And Jays* (1995: Sierra Club Books)

Sierra Magazine – *Groundhog Ways*: January / February 2010

Paul Theroux – *Last Train To Zona Verde: My Ultimate African Safari* (2013: Houghton Mifflin Harcourt)

Joel Thomas – *Creature Comforts: Wildlife Stories & Solutions* (2010: CreateSpace)

William W. Warner – *Beautiful Swimmers: Watermen, Crabs, And The Chesapeake Bay* (1976: Little Brown & Co.)

Peter Watkins and Jonathan Stockland – *Winged Wonders: A Celebration of Birds in Human History* (2007: Blue Bridge)

Dick Wolfsie – *Mornings with Barney: The True Story Of An Extraordinary Beagle* (2009: Skyhorse Pub.)

CPSIA information can be obtained
at www.ICGtesting.com
Printed in the USA
FFOW03n1153210216
21691FF